D1798708

GOLDEN NUGGETS

OF

THOUGHT

VOLUME III

Compiled

By

EZRA L. MARLER

Bookcraft
Salt Lake City, Utah

24th Printing, 1993

Lithographed in the United States of America
PUBLISHERS PRESS
Salt Lake City, Utah

CONTENTS

Adversity and Affliction 7

Age 12

Anger 13

Aspirations and Ideals 14

Brotherhood 17

Character—Nobility 19

Courage 26

Culture 27

Death and Immortality 29

Deity and Divinity 30

Duty 40

Envy 41

Example and Influence 42

Faith—Hope—Confidence 46

Fear 50

Freedom and Free Agency 51

Friends—Friendliness 52

Giving 54

Gratitude 55

Happiness—Joy 57

Helpfulness 60

Home and Family 64

Humility 70

CONTENTS

Justice—Judgment 70
Kindness 72
Life and Living 75
Light and Learning 93
Mother 96
Opportunity 98
Patriotism 99
Peace—Peacemakers 101
Prayer 102
Procrastination 107
Proverbs and Psalms 109
Religion 118
Reverence 122
Rewards of Righteous Living 123
Repentance and Forgiveness 127
Riches 127
Salvation and Exaltation 132
Sentence Sermons of Dr. Karl G. Maeser 154
Success 133
Thrift 135
Truth—Honesty 136
Values of Life 138
Wickedness—Sin 142
Woman 146
Work—Industry 152

ADVERSITY AND AFFLICTION

WORTH WHILE

It is easy enough to be pleasant,
  When life flows by like a song,
But the man worth while is one who will smile,
  When everything goes dead wrong.
For the test of the heart is trouble,
  And it always comes with the years,
And the smile that is worth the praises of earth
  Is the smile that shines through tears.

It is easy enough to be prudent,
  When nothing tempts you to stray,
When without or within no voice of sin
  Is luring your soul away;
But it's only a negative virtue
  Until it is tried by fire,
And the life that is worth the praises of earth
  Is the one that resists desire.

By the cynic, the sad, the fallen,
  Who had no strength for the strife,
The world's highway is cumbered to-day;
  They make up the sum of life.

But the virtue that conquers passion,
  And the sorrow that hides in a smile,
It is these that are worth the homage on earth
  For we find them but once in a while.
                    —*Ella Wheeler Wilcox.*

Triumphs without difficulties are empty. Indeed, it is difficulties that make the triumph. It is no feat to travel the smooth road.—*Anon.*

There are nuggets of gold in Moses that would never have been found had he remained in Pharaoh's palace. It took forty years of roughing it to bring them to the surface.
                    —*E. P. Brown.*

Adversity is necessary to the development of man's virtue.
                    —*"Wisdom of the Chinese."*

  I walked a mile with Pleasure,
    She chatted me all the way,
  But I was none the wiser
    For what she had to say.

I walked a mile with Sorrow,
    And ne'er a word said she,
But O the things I learned from her
    When Sorrow walked with me!
                    —*Anonymous.*

If you would not have affliction visit you twice, listen at once to what it teaches.
                    —*James Burgh.*

THE OBSTACLE ALWAYS AHEAD

There's always a river to cross,
    Always an effort to make,
If there's anything good to win,
    Any rich prize to take.
Yonder's the fruit we crave;
    Yonder the charming scene;
But deep and wide, with a troubled tide,
    Is the river that lies between.

For rougher the way that we take,
    The stouter the heart and the nerve;

The stones in our path we break,
  Nor e'er from our impulse swerve;
For the glory we hope to win
  Our labors we count no loss;
'Tis folly to pause and murmur because
  Of the river we have to cross.

                    —*Anonymous.*

God carries many of his children into the darkened rooms of affliction, and when they come forth again there is more of the beauty of Christ in their souls. We get many of the best things of our lives out of suffering and pain. It may be the easiest, but it surely is not the best life and the most blessed that is free from trial. The crown is not given to untried lives.

                    —*Dr. J. R. Miller.*

YOUR PRACTICE

Do not quarrel with your lot in life. Do not complain of its never-ceasing cares, its environment, the vexations you have to stand, the small and sordid souls you have to live and work with. Above all, do not resent temptation; do not be perplexed because it seems to thicken around you more and more, and ceases neither for effort nor for agony nor prayer. That is your practice. That is the practice which God appoints you. And it is having its work in making you patient, and humble, and generous, and unselfish, and kind, and courteous.   —*Henry Drummond*.

ADVERSITY A BLESSING

A smooth sea never made a skilful mariner, neither do uninterrupted prosperity and success qualify for usefulness and happiness. The storms of adversity, like those of the ocean, rouse the faculties, and excite the invention, prudence, skill and fortitude of the voyager.—*Anonymous*.

Once there lived an old woman who was always so cheerful that everyone wondered at her: "But you must have some clouds in your life," said a visitor. "Clouds?" she replied, "why, of course; if there were no clouds, where would the blessed showers come from?"

—*Sunshine Magazine*.
"*Mutual Moments*."

AGE

YOU TELL ME I AM GETTING OLD . . .

———

You tell me I am getting old.
I tell you that's not so!
The "house" I live in is worn out, and that, of
      course, I know.
It's been in use a long, long while; it's weathered
      many a gale;
I'm really not surprised you think it's getting
      somewhat frail.

The color changing on the roof, the windows
      getting dim,
The walls a bit transparent and looking rather
      thin,
The foundation not so steady as once it used to
      be—
My "house" is getting shaky, but my "house"
      isn't ME!

My few short years can't make me old. I feel
      I'm in my youth.
Eternity lies just ahead, a life of joy and truth.

I'm going to live forever, there; life will go on—
        it's grand!
You tell me I am getting old? You just don't
        understand.

The dweller in my little "house" is young and
        bright and gay;
Just starting on a life to last throughout eternal
        day.
You only see the outside, which is all that most
        folks see.
You tell me I am getting old?
You've mixed my "house" with ME!
        —by *Dora Johnson* (88 years young).

ANGER

Note: Opinions differ. Take your choice.

Every great sin ought to arouse a great anger.
Mob law is better than no law at all. A community which rises in its wrath to punish with misdirected anger a great wrong is in a healthier moral condition than a community which looks upon its perpetration with apathy and unconcern.
        —*Lyman Abbott.*

Do not teach your children never to be angry; teach them how to be angry and sin not.

—*Lymann Abbott.*

Nothing is improved by anger, unless it be the arch of a cat's back. A man with his back up is spoiling his figure. People look none the handsomer for being red in the face. It takes a great deal out of a man to get into a towering rage; it is almost as unhealthy as having a fit. . . . Whatever wrong I suffer, it can not do me half so much hurt as being angry about it.   —*Spurgeon.*

ASPIRATIONS AND IDEALS

Christianity helped to make Angelo and Raphael by furnishing them with grand themes. As no lips can be eloquent unless they are speaking in the name of a great truth, so no painter can paint unless some one brings him a great subject. Heaven and hell made the poet, Dante. Christianity made Beatrice. Paradise made John Milton. The mother of our Lord and the last judgment made Angelo. It is the great theme that makes the orator, the painter, the poet. The great theme lifts up the soul and makes it the revealer of a new world.   —*Swing.*

I mean to make myself a man, and if I succeed in that, I shall succeed in everything.

—*James A. Garfield.*

Where'er a noble deed is wrought,
Where'er is spoken a noble thought,
Our hearts in glad surprise
To higher levels rise.
—*Henry Wadsworth Longfellow.*

Keep your mind on the great and splendid things you would like to do and then, as the days go gliding by you will find yourself unconsciously seizing the opportunities that are required for the fulfillment of your desire. Picture in your mind the able, earnest, useful person you desire to be, and the thought you hold is hourly transforming you into that particular individual you so admire.

—*Elbert Hubbard.*

Life is a sheet of paper white,
Whereon each one of us may write
His word or two, and then comes night.

Greatly begin! Though thou have time
But for a line, be that sublime—
Not failure, but low aim, is crime.
—*James Russell Lowell.*

One thing I do, forgetting those things which are behind, and reaching forth unto those things which are before, I press toward the mark for the prize of the high calling of God in Christ Jesus.
—*Paul*, Phil. 3:13-14.

Build on, and make thy castles high and fair,
 Rising and reaching upward to the skies;
Listen to voices in the upper air,
 Nor lose thy simple faith in mysteries.
—*Henry Wadsworth Longfellow.*

Four things a man must learn to do
If he would make his record true:
 To think, without confusion, clearly;
 To act, from honest motives, purely;
 To love his fellow man sincerely,
 To trust in God and heaven securely.
—*Henry Van Dyke.*

Ah, but a man's reach should exceed his grasp
Else what's a heaven for?   —*Browning.*

One little hour of watching with the Master,
 Eternal years to walk with Him in white;
One little hour to bravely meet disaster,
 Eternal years to reign with Him in light;

One little hour of weary toils and trials,
   Eternal years for calm and peaceful rest;
One little hour for patient self-denials,
   Eternal years for life, where life is blest.

                              —Anonymous.

The ideal life is in our blood and never will be
still. Sad will be the day for any man when he
becomes contented with the thoughts he is thinking and the deeds he is doing—where there is not
forever beating at the doors of his soul some great
desire to do something larger, which he knows he
was meant and made to do.   *—Anonymous.*

BROTHERHOOD

WORLD BROTHERHOOD

My country is the world;
My flag with stars impearled
   Fills all the skies.
All the round earth I claim,
Peoples of every name
And all inspiring fame
   My heart would prize.

And all men are my kin,
Since every man has been
  Blood of my blood.
I glory in the grace
And strength of every race,
And joy in every trace
  Of brotherhood.

The days of pack and clan
Shall yield to love of man,
  When war flags are furled;
We shall be done with hate,
And strife of state with state,
When man with man shall mate,
  O'er all the world.

—Anonymous.

A MESSAGE OF LOVE

I'm sending a thought on the vibrant air:
"I love people everywhere,"
People old and people young,
People of a foreign tongue;
I care not who nor where they are,
My love shall reach the highest star,

The lowest hut, the strongest cell—
Where'er the sons of God may dwell.
                              —*Vivian Y. Laramore.*

CHARACTER—NOBILITY

NOBILITY

True worth is in *being*, not *seeming*—
   In doing, each day that goes by,
Some little good—not in dreaming
   Of great things to do by and by.
For whatever men say in their blindness,
   And in spite of the fancies of youth,
There's nothing so kingly as kindness,
   And nothing so royal as truth.

We get back our mete as we measure—
   We cannot do wrong and feel right,
Nor can we give pain and gain pleasure,
   For justice avenges each slight.
The air for the wing of the sparrow,
   The bush for the robin and wren,
But always the path that is narrow
   And straight, for the children of men.
                              —*Alice Cary.*

A man should not allow himself to hate even his enemies; because if you indulge this passion on some occasion, it will rise of itself on others. If you hate your enemies, you will contract such a vicious habit of mind as by degrees will break out upon those who are your friends, or those who are indifferent to you.   —*Plutarch.*

> We all are blind until we see
>   That in the human plan
> Nothing is worth the making if
>   It does not make the man.
>
> Why build these cities glorious
>   If man unbuilded goes?
> In vain we build the world, unless
>   The builder also grows.
>
>   —*Anonymous.*

The spirit of self-help is the root of all genuine growth in the individual; and, exhibited in the lives of many, it constitutes the true source of national vigor and strength. Help from without is often enfeebling in its effects, but help from within invariably invigorates. —*Samuel Smiles.*

It is not difficult to get away into retirement, and there live upon your own convictions; nor is it difficult to mix with men and follow their convictions; but to enter into the world, and there live firmly and fearlessly according to your own conscience, that is Christian greatness.

—*Anonymous.*

THE UPPER ROAD

I'm going by the upper road,
  For that still holds the sun;
I'm climbing through night's pastures
  Where the starry rivers run;
If you should think to seek me
  In my old dark abode,
You'll find this writing on the door:
  "He's on the Upper Road."

—*Anonymous.*

Reading makes a full man, conversation a ready man, and writing an exact man.   —*Bacon.*

The man of worth is really great without being proud; the mean man is proud without being really great.   —*"Wisdom of the Chinese."*

"When you die, all that you have will go to another; all that you are will be yours forever."

Thou must be true thyself,
  If thou the truth wouldst teach;
Thy soul must overflow, if thou
  Another soul wouldst reach.
It needs the overflow of heart
  To give the lips full speech.

Think truly, and thy thoughts
  Shall the world's famine feed.
Speak truly, and each word of thine
  Shall be a faithful seed.
Live truly, and thy life shall be
  A great and noble creed.
                    —*Horatius Bonar.*

This above all: to thine own self be true,
And it must follow as the night the day,
Thou canst not then be false to any man.
                    —*William Shakespeare.*

We learn wisdom from failure much more than
from success. We often discover what will do by
finding out what will not do; and probably he
who never made a mistake never made a discovery.
                    —*Samuel Smiles.*

Do not think that what your thoughts dwell upon is of no matter. Your thoughts are making you. —*Bishop Steere.*

BE STRONG

Be strong!
We are not here to play, to dream, to drift;
We have hard work to do, and loads to lift;
Shun not the struggle—face it; 'tis God's gift.

Be strong!
Say not, "The days are evil. Who's to blame?"
And fold the hands and acquiesce—oh shame!
Stand up, speak out, and bravely, in God's name.

Be strong!
It matters not how deep intrenched the wrong,
How hard the battle goes, the day how long;
Faint not—fight on! Tomorrow comes the song.
—*Maltbie Davenport Babcock.*

A man is not bad because a viper bites him. Excellent persons are liable to be assailed by malicious slanderers, who, because of their serpent nature, take delight in attacking the good. An apostle once had a viper fasten upon his hand, but he shook it off into the fire, and it did him no harm.   —*Spurgeon.*

INVICTUS

Out of the night that covers me,
  Black as the Pit from pole to pole,
I thank whatever gods may be
  For my unconquerable soul.

In the fell clutch of circumstance
  I have not winced nor cried aloud.
Under the bludgeonings of chance
  My head is bloody, but unbowed.

Beyond this place of wrath and tears
  Looms but the Horror of the shade,
And yet the menace of the years
  Finds, and shall find, me unafraid.

It matters not how strait the gate,
  How charged with punishments the scroll,
I am the master of my fate;
  I am the captain of my soul.
                                   —*William E. Henley.*

It is a good and safe rule to sojourn in every place as if you meant to spend your life there, never omitting an opportunity of doing a kindness, or speaking a true word, or making a friend.

—*Ruskin.*

Be such a man, and live such a life,
That if every man were such as you,
And every life a life like yours,
This earth would be God's Paradise.
—*Phillips Brooks.*

BEING TRUE TO OURSELVES

Our great and most difficult duty, as social beings, is . . . to open our minds to the thoughts and persuations of others, and yet to hold fast the sacred right of private judgment; to receive impulses from our fellow beings, and yet to act from our own souls; to sympathise with others and yet to determine our own feelings; to act with others, and yet to follow our own conscience; to unite social deference and self-dominion.

—*W. E. Channing.*

DO WHAT IS RIGHT

———

Do what is right; the day-dawn is breaking,
Hailing a future of freedom and light;
Angels above us are silent notes taking
Of every action; do what is right!

Do what is right, let the consequence follow;
Battle for freedom in spirit and might;
And with stout hearts look ye forth till tomorrow;
God will protect you; do what is right!

—Anon.

———

COURAGE

Have not I commanded thee? Be strong and of a good courage; be not afraid, neither be thou dismayed; for the Lord thy God is with thee whithersoever thou goest.   *—Joshua* 1:9.

Let us have faith that right makes might; and in that faith let us, to the end, dare to do our duty as we understand it.   *—Abraham Lincoln.*

CULTURE

See some good picture—in nature, if possible, or on canvas—hear a page of the best music, or read a great poem every day. You will always find a free half hour for one or the other, and at the end of the year your mind will shine with such an accumulation of jewels as will astonish even yourself. —*Henry Wadsworth Longfellow.*

Learning makes a man fit company for himself as well as for others. —*Anonymous.*

In all the affairs of life, social as well as political, courtesies of a small and trivial character are the ones which strike deepest to the grateful and appreciating heart. —*Henry Clay.*

The books which help you most are those which make you think most. The hardest way of learning is by easy reading; but a great book that comes from a great thinker is a ship of thought, deep freighted with truth and beauty.

—*Theodore Parker.*

If you would not be forgotten as soon as you are dead, either write things worth reading or do things worth writing. —*Benjamin Franklin.*

THE LOVE OF BOOKS

When a man loves books he has in him that which will console him under many sorrows and strengthen him in various trials. Such a love will keep him at home, and make his time pass pleasantly. Even when visited by bodily or mental affliction he can resort to this book-love and be cured. . . . And when a man is at home and happy with a book, sitting by his fireside, he must be a churl if he does not communicate that happiness. Let him read now and then to his wife and children. Those thoughts will grow and take root in the hearts and minds of his listeners. A man who feels sympathy with what is good and noble, is at the time he feels that sympathy, good and noble himself.   —*J. H. Friswell.*

DEATH AND IMMORTALITY

Fast as the rolling seasons bring
　　The hour of fate to those we love,
Each pearl that leaves the broken string
　　Is set in Friendship's crown above.

As narrower grows the earthly chain
  The circle widens in the sky;
These are our treasures that remain,
  But those are stars that beam on high.
                              —O. W. Holmes.

CROSSING THE BAR

Sunset and evening star,
  And one clear call for me,
And may there be no moaning at the bar,
  When I put out to sea.

Twilight and evening bell,
  And after that the dark!
And may there be no sadness of farewell,
  When I embark.

For tho' from out our bourne of time and place
  The flood may bear me far,
I hope to see my Pilot face to face
  When I have crossed the bar.
                              —Alfred Tennyson.

MOURN NOT FOR THE DEAD

Mourn not the dead who calmly lie
　　By God's own hand composed to rest;
For, hark! A voice from yonder sky
　　Proclaims them blest—supremely blest.
With them the toil and strife are o'er;
　　Their labors end, their sorrows cease;
For they have gained the blissful shore
　　Where dwells serene eternal peace.
—J. Lotton.

"When death overtakes us, all that we have is left to others; all that we are we take with us."

DEITY AND DIVINITY

THE COMING OF CHRIST AMONG THE NEPHITES

And behold the third time they did understand the voice which they heard; and it said unto them: Behold my Beloved Son, in whom I am well pleased, in whom I have glorified my name—hear ye him.

And it came to pass, as they understood they cast their eyes up again towards heaven; and behold, they saw a Man descending out of heaven; and he was clothed in a white robe; and he came down and stood in the midst of them;

And it came to pass that he stretched forth his hand and spake unto the people, saying:

Behold, I am Jesus Christ, whom the prophets testified shall come into the world.

And behold, I am the light and the life of the world;   —*III Nephi* 11:6-10.

Therefore, I would that ye should behold that the Lord truly did teach the people, for the space of three days; and after that he did show himself unto them oft, and did break bread oft, and bless it, and give it unto them.   —*III Nephi* 26:13.

O remember, remember, my sons, the words which king Benjamin spake unto his people; yea, remember that there is no other way nor means whereby man can be saved, only through the atoning blood of Jesus Christ.   —*Helaman* 5:9.

NOT MINE, BUT THINE

———

All those who journey soon or late
Must pass within the garden's gate;
Must kneel alone in darkness there,
And battle with some fierce despair.
God pity those who cannot say:
"Not mine, but Thine"; who only pray
"Let this cup pass," and can not see
The purpose in Gethsemane.
—*Ella Wheeler Wilcox.*

For unto us a child is born, unto us a son is given; and the government shall be upon his shoulder; and his name shall be called, Wonderful, Counsellor, The Mighty God, The Everlasting Father, The Prince of Peace.

Of the increase of his government and peace there shall be no end, upon the throne of David, and upon his kingdom, to order it, and to establish it with judgment and with justice from henceforth even for ever. The zeal of the Lord of hosts will perform this.   —*Is.* 9:6-7.

JESUS CHRIST

—

"Alexander, Caesar, Charlemagne and myself founded empires; but on what foundation did we rest the creatures of our genius? Upon force. But Jesus Christ founded an empire upon love; and at this hour millions of men would die for Him.

"I die before my time, and my body will be given back to the earth to become food for worms. Such is the fate of him who has been called the 'great Napoleon.' What an abyss between my deep misery and the eternal kingdom of Christ, which is proclaimed, loved, adored and is still existing over the whole earth!"

—Napoleon Bonaparte.

No true work since the world began was ever wasted; no true life since the world began has ever failed. Oh, understand those two perverted words, "failure" and "success" and measure them by the eternal, not the earthly, standard. When after thirty obscure, toilsome, unrecorded years in the shop of the village carpenter, one came forth to be pre-eminently the man of sorrows, to wander from city to city in homeless labors, and to expire in lonely agony upon the shameful cross—was that a failure?   —*F. W. Farrar.*

But now mine own eyes have beheld God; but not my natural, but my spiritual eyes, for my natural eyes could not have beheld; for I should have withered and died in his presence; and I beheld his face, for I was transfigured before him.
                    —*P. of G. P., Moses* 1:11.

CHRIST WITH US MEANS THE CROSS FOR US

———

When God breaks up your plans, and throws you to the very ground, and breaks all the threads in the loom which you are weaving, and says to you, "Begin again," is there any Christ for you at that point of your overthrow? Can you go forth unto your Savior marking that place in His life where He was overthrown, identifying it in some way with your own overthrow? Can you stand rejoicing in Christ at that very point of humiliation and crucifixion? Christ may be followed in two ways—victorious, and in disgrace and ignominy;

and we are called to follow, first, not Christ as He is set forth in all the royalty of philosophy and reason, but a Christ humiliated, a Christ despised; a Christ hated, a Christ crucified. Before we stand with Christ upon Olivet we must stand with Him on Calvary—must walk with him thither.

—Beecher.

Wherefore, all things which are good cometh of God; and that which is evil cometh of the devil; for the devil is an enemy unto God, and fighteth against him continually, and inviteth and enticeth to sin, and to do that which is evil continually.

But behold, that which is of God inviteth and enticeth to do good continually.

—Moroni 7:12-13.

JESUS, ONCE OF HUMBLE BIRTH

Jesus, once of humble birth,
Now in glory comes to earth;
Once He suffered grief and pain,
Now he comes on earth to reign.

Once a meek and lowly lamb,
Now the Lord, the great I Am;
Once upon the cross He bowed,
Now his chariot is the cloud.

Once He groaned in blood and tears,
Now in glory He appears;
Once rejected by His own,
Now their King He shall be known.

Once forsaken, left alone,
Now exalted to a throne;
Once all things He meekly bore,
But He now will bear no more.
—*Parley P. Pratt.*

HE KNOWS

For reasons quite unknown to us, God often calls the young,
Whose futures seem so promising; whose success has just begun!
God has a plan for every man and by that Plan, we live.
He has the power to take away—He has the power to give.

"Blessed are the ones who mourn," for they shall
  surely find
That God will comfort us through faith and give
  us peace of mind.

                                —*Aletha Packard.*

THE FATHER AND THE SON
APPEAR TO MAN

. . . just at this moment of great alarm, I saw a
pillar of light exactly over my head, above the
brightness of the sun, which descended gradually
until it fell upon me.

It no sooner appeared than I found myself de-
livered from the enemy which held me bound.
When the light rested upon me I saw two Person-
ages, whose brightness and glory defy all descrip-
tion, standing above me in the air. One of them
spake unto me, calling me by name and said,
pointing to the other—"*This is My Beloved Son.
Hear Him.*"   —*Joseph Smith.*

            "*History of the Church*" *v. 1, p. 5.*

But behold, all things have been done in the
wisdom of him who knoweth all things.

                                —*II Ne.* 2:24.

ETERNAL PROGRESS

———

We believe in a God who is in himself progressive, whose majesty is intelligence; whose perfection consists in eternal advancement; the perpetual work of whose creation stands "finished yet renewed forever"—a Being who has attained his exalted state by a path which now his children follow; whose glory it is their heritage to share. In spite of the opposition of other sects, in the face of direct charges of blasphemy, the Church proclaims the eternal truth, "As man is, God once was; as God is, man may become." With such a future, well may man open his heart to the stream of revelation, past, present and to come.

—*Dr. James E. Talmage.*

THE HEART OF THE ETERNAL

———

There's a wideness in God's mercy,
  Like the wideness of the sea;
There's a kindness in his justice,
  Which is more than liberty.

For the love of God is broader
  Than the measures of man's mind;
And the heart of the Eternal
  Is most wonderfully kind.

If our love were but more simple,
  We should take him at his word,
And our lives would all be sunshine
  In the sweetness of our Lord.
                              —*Frederick W. Faber.*

DIVINE MESSAGES

Day and night, and every moment, there are
voices about us. All the hours speak as they pass;
and in every event there is a message to us; and
all our circumstances talk with us; but it is in
divine language, that worldliness misunderstands,
that selfishness is frightened at, and that only the
children of God hear rightly and happily.
                              —*William Mountford.*

A common thing is a grass blade small,
  Crushed by the feet that pass,

But all the dwarfs and giants tall,
  Working till doomsday shadows fall
Can't make a blade of grass.
            —*J. S. Cutler's* "Wonderful."
                  "Mutual Moments."

The man who loves God, loves also the man whom God loves.   —*Anon.*

DUTY

THERE'S HEAVEN IN IT

———

We turn our sad, reluctant gaze
  Upon the path of duty;
Its barren, uninviting ways
  Are void of bloom and beauty.
Yet in that road, though dark and cold
  It seems as we begin it,
As we press on—lo! we behold
  There's heaven in it.
              —*Ella Wheeler Wilcox.*

Our grand business is, not to see what lies dimly at a distance, but to do what lies closely at hand.

Do the duty which lieth nearest to thee, which thou knowest to be a duty. Thy second duty will already have become clearer. —*Thomas Carlyle.*

THE DUTY OF THE HOUR

———

Don't waste life in doubts and fears; spend yourself on the work before you, well assured that the right performance of this hour's duties will be the best preparation for the hours or ages that follow it.   —*Ralph W. Emerson.*

ENVY

DON'T ENVY OTHER FOLKS

———

Don't think when you have troubles
    That your neighbor goes scot-free
Because he shows a smiling front
    And battles cheerfully.
No, Man! He, too, has troubles,
    But herein the difference lies,
While you go idly moping round,
    The other fellow tries.

Don't envy other people;
  Maybe, if the truth you knew,
You'd find their burdens heavier far
  Than is the case with you.
Because a fellow, rain or shine,
  Can show a smiling face,
Don't think you'd have an easier time
  If you could take his place.

'Tis hope and cheery courage
  That incite one to retrieve
One's past mistakes, to start afresh,
  To dare and to achieve.
So smile, and if perchance you light
  The spark of hope anew
In some poor sad and burdened heart,
  All honor be to you.

                    —*Anonymous.*

EXAMPLE AND INFLUENCE

In so far as you approach temptation to a man, you do him an injury; and if he is overcome, you share his guilt.   —*Samuel Johnson.*

Train up a child in the way he should go; and
when he is old, he will not depart from it.

—*Prov.* 22:6.

THE IMMORTALITY OF INFLUENCE

We scatter seeds with careless hand,
  And dream we ne'er shall see them more;
    But for a thousand years
    Their fruit appears,
In weeds that mar the land,
    Or healthful store.

The deeds we do, the words we say,
  Into still air do seem to fleet;
    We count them ever past,
    But they shall last.
In the dread judgment they
    And we shall meet.

—*Keble.*

If you want your neighbor to see what the
Christ spirit will do for him, let him see what it
has done for you.   —*Henry Ward Beecher.*

THE ARROW AND THE SONG

I shot an arrow into the air,
It fell to earth, I knew not where;
For, so swiftly it flew, the sight
Could not follow it in its flight.

I breathed a song into the air,
It fell to earth, I knew not where;
For who has sight so keen and strong
That it can follow the flight of song?

Long, long afterward, in an oak
I found the arrow, still unbroke;
And the song, from beginning to end,
I found again in the heart of a friend.
                    — *Henry W. Longfellow.*

I am a part of all whom I have met.
                    —*Alfred Tennyson.*

No man or woman of humblest sort can really
be strong, gentle, pure and good without somebody
being helped and comforted by the very existence
of that goodness.   —*Phillips Brooks.*

The best way for a man to train up a child in the way he should go is to travel that way himself.

—*Anonymous.*

GOOD COMPANY

Try to frequent the company of your betters. In books and life, that is the most wholesome society; learn to admire rightly; the great pleasure of life is that. Note what great men admired; they admired great things; narrow spirits admire basely and worship meanly.   —*Thackery.*

A BETTER WORLD

Do you wish the world were better?
  Let me tell you what to do:
Set a watch upon your actions,
  Keep them always straight and true;
Rid your mind of selfish motives;
  Let your thoughts be clean and high;
You can make a little Eden
  Of the sphere you occupy.

—*Anonymous.*

FAITH—HOPE—CONFIDENCE

Faith is the vision of the heart; it sees God in the dark as well as in the day.   —*Anon.*

Our doubts are traitors, and make us lose the good we oft might win, by fearing the attempt.
                    —*William Shakespeare.*

NEW EVERY MORNING

———

Every day is a fresh beginning;
  Every morn is a world made new.
You, who are weary of sorrow and sinning,
  Here is a beautiful hope for you—
  A hope for me and a hope for you.

Yesterday is a part of forever,
  Bound up in a sheaf, which God holds tight—
With glad days and sad days and bad days, which
    never
  Shall visit us more with their bloom and their
    blight,
  Their fullness of sunshine and sorrowful night.

Isn't it strange how long a night can grow
  Ere morning and the dew?
Isn't it queer how black a cloud can blow
  Before the sun breaks through?
Faith is remembering ere break of day,
  Or ere the storm is done,
That out of somewhere speeding on their way
  Are the morning and the sun! —*Anonymous*.

OLD AND NEW

Oh, sometimes gleams upon our sight,
Through present wrong, the eternal right;
And step by step, since time began,
We see the steady gain of man.

That all of good the past hath had
Remains to make our own time glad,
Our common, daily life divine
And every land a Palestine.

Through the harsh noises of our day
A low, sweet prelude finds its way;
Through clouds of doubt and creeds of fear
A light is breaking, calm and clear.
                        —*Anonymous*.

An old colored brother is said to have finished his prayer with words like these: "And now good Lord, I know that you aint goen to let nothing come to me that me and you together can't handle."

Passive Faith but praises in the light,
　　When sun doth shine.
Active Faith will praise in darkest night—
　　Which faith is thine?
　　　　　　　　　—Anonymous.

TODAY

Let them go, since we can not recall them;
　　Can not find and can not atone.
God in His mercy receive, forgive them!
　　Only the new days are our own—
　　Today is ours, and today alone.

Every day is a fresh beginning!
　　Listen, my soul, to the glad refrain,
And in spite of old sorrow and older sinning
　　And puzzles forecasted and possible pain,
　　Take heart with the day, and begin again.
　　　　　　　　　—Susan Coolidge.

Unanswered yet? Faith cannot be unanswered.
Her feet are firmly planted on the Rock;
Amid the wildest storms she stands undaunted
Nor quails before the loudest thunder shock.
She knows Omnipotence has heard her prayer,
And cries, "It shall be done, sometime, some-
  where."

—Mrs. Ophelia G. Adams.

HE THAT BELIEVETH

He that believeth shall not make haste,
In useless hurry his strength to waste;
Who walks with God can afford to wait,
For he can never arrive too late.

He that believeth shall not delay;
Who carries the word of the King on its way
Keeps pace with the Pleiades' marching tune
And he can never arrive too soon.

He that believeth shall walk serene,
With ordered steps and leisured mien;
He dwells in the midst of eternities,
And the timeless ages of God are his.

—Annie J. Flint.

There are some who forget that the laws of the spiritual world are no less inflexible and inviolable than those of the physical world; that conduct is everything; and that the faith which saves, and which, working by love, makes conduct, is something much deeper and more substantial than the muttering of an unfelt creed, or than the melancholy presumption that to think ourselves saved is by itself a passport into the everlasting habitations.   —*Bishop Thorold.*

FEAR

WHY SHOULD I FEAR?

Why should I fear?
To know that God is near,
    Gives calm assurance in the darkest hour;
By night or day,
If I but humbly pray,
    I feel the presence of His mighty power.

Why should I fear?
I know that God can hear,
  And watches o'er me from His throne above;
If I do good
And serve Him as I should,
  My heart is filled with joy and peace and love.
                              —*Bessie B. Decker.*

An Arab folk tale relates that Pestilence once met a caravan upon the desert-way to Baghdad. "Why," asked the Arab chief, "must you hasten to Baghdad?"

"To take 5,000 lives," Pestilence replied.

Upon the way back from the city of the Caliphs, Pestilence and the caravan met again. "You deceived me," the chief said angrily. "Instead of 5,000 lives, you took 50,000!"

"Nay," said Pestilence. "Five thousand and not one more. It was Fear who killed the rest."

                    —*Maurice Duhamel* in
                      "They Tell a Story."

FREEDOM AND FREE AGENCY

There are two freedoms—the false, where a man is free to do what he likes; the true, where a man is free to do what he ought. —*Charles Kingsley.*

Conquer thyself. Till thou hast done that, thou art a slave; for it is almost as well to be in subjection to another's appetite as thine own.

—Burton.

. . . I know that he granteth unto men according to their desire, whether it be unto death or unto life; yea, I know that he allotteth unto men according to their wills, whether they be unto salvation or unto destruction.

Yea, and I know that good and evil have come before all men; he that knoweth not good from evil is blameless; but he that knoweth good and evil, to him it is given according to his desires, whether he desireth good or evil, life or death, joy or remorse of conscience.   *—Alma* 29:1-4.

FRIENDS—FRIENDLINESS

Life is sweet because of the friends we have made
And the things which in common we share;
We want to live on, not because of ourselves
But because of the ones who would care.
It's living and doing for somebody else—
On that, all of life's splendor depends,

And the joy of it all, when we count it all up,
Is found in the making of friends.

—*Anonymous.*

Forming resentments with mankind may be called "planting misery"; putting aside virtuous deeds, instead of practicing them, may be called "robbing oneself."   —*"Wisdom of the Chinese."*

If a man does not receive guests at home, he will meet with very few hosts abroad.

—*"Wisdom of the Chinese."*

The only way to have a friend is to be one.

—*Emerson.*

The friend in my adversity I shall always cherish most. I can better trust those who helped to relieve the gloom of my dark hours than those who are so ready to enjoy with me the sunshine of my prosperity.   —*Ulysses S. Grant.*

A man should choose a friend who is better than himself. There are plenty of acquaintances in the world, but very few real friends.

—*"Wisdom of the Chinese."*

Win new friends but keep the old.
The first are silver, the latter gold.
                              —*Anon.*

Tact is the knack of making a point without making an enemy.   —*Howard W. Newton.*

A good deed is never lost; he who sows courtesy reaps friendship, and he who plants kindness gathers love.   —*Anonymous.*

GIVING

Success thinks in terms of giving, not getting. The business man who thinks only of returns, soon finds himself without friends among his prospects and customers.   —*Anon.*

I gave a beggar from my little store
    Of well earned gold.
He spent the shining ore, and came again and yet
        again
    Still cold and hungry as before.
I gave a thought, and through that thought of
        mine

He found himself, the man, supreme, divine!
Fed, clothed and crowned with blessings manifold,
   And now he begs no more.
                    —*Ella Wheeler Wilcox.*

Give 'what you have to some one; it may be
better than you dare to think.   —*Longfellow.*

GRATITUDE

THE THANKFUL HEART

For all that God in mercy sends—
For health and children, home and friends;
For comforts in the time of need,
For every kindly word or deed,
For happy thoughts and holy talk,
For guidance in our daily walk—
In everything give thanks!

For the sweet sleep which comes with night,
For the returning morning light,
For the bright sun that shines on high,
For the stars glittering in the sky—
For these and every thing we see,
O Lord, our hearts we lift to Thee;
In every thing give thanks!
                    —*E. I. Tupper.*

And thus we can behold how false, and also the unsteadiness of the hearts of the children of men; yea, we can see that the Lord in his great infinite goodness doth bless and prosper those who put their trust in him.

Yea, and we may see at the very time when he doth prosper his people, yea in the increase of their fields, their flocks and their herds, and in gold, and in silver, and in all manner of precious things of every kind and art; sparing their lives, and delivering them out of the hands of their enemies; softening the hearts of their enemies that they should not declare wars against them; yea, and in fine, doing all things for the welfare and happiness of his people; yea, then is the time that they do harden their hearts, and do forget the Lord their God, and do trample under their feet the Holy One—yea, and this because of their ease, and their exceedingly great prosperity.

—Helaman 12:1-2.

I say unto you, my brethren, that if you should render all the thanks and praise which your whole soul has power to possess, to that God who has created you, and has kept and preserved you, and has caused that ye should rejoice, and has granted that ye should live in peace one with another—

I say unto you that if ye should serve him who has created you from the beginning, and is preserving you from day to day, by lending you breath, that ye may live and move and do according to your own will, and even supporting you from one moment to another—I say, if ye should serve him with all your whole souls yet ye would be unprofitable servants.

—*Mosiah* 2:20-21.

HAPPINESS—JOY

And if it so be that you should labor all your days in crying repentance unto this people and bring, save it be one soul unto me, how great shall be your joy with him in the kingdom of my Father!

And now, if your joy will be great with one soul that you have brought unto me into the kingdom of my Father, how great will be your joy if you should bring many souls unto me!

—*D. & C.* 18:15-16.

To the contented, even poverty and obscurity bring happiness, while to the ambitious, wealth and honors are productive of misery.

—"Wisdom of the Chinese."

It takes so little to make us glad;
Just a cheering clasp of a friendly hand,
Just a word from one who can understand,
And we finish the task we long had planned,
And we lose the doubt and the fear we had—
So little it takes to make us glad.

—Anonymous.

Adam fell that men might be; and men are, that they might have joy.   *—II Nephi* 3:24-25.

Happiness is the object and design of our existence; and will be the end thereof, if we pursue the path that leads to it; and that path is virtue,   uprightness, faithfulness, holiness, and keeping all the commandments of God.

—"Teachings of Joseph Smith." p. 255.

When life seems just a dreary grind,
    And things seem fated to annoy,
Say something nice to someone else
    And watch the world light up with joy.

—Anonymous.

THE PROBLEM OF LIFE

There are so many possibilities in life, in attainment and achievement, and so many opportunities of doing good, that it is a glorious thing to live. Surely, then, we ought to make the most of our life.

The ideal life is one of joy. The face ought to be shining—shining even in darkness. People say this is a sad world, yes, for those who have eyes only for shadows. He who has songs in his heart hears songs wherever he goes.

Dr. J. R. Miller.

CHEERFULNESS

Nothing on earth can smile but man. Gems may flash reflected light; but what is a diamond flash compared with an eye flash? Flowers cannot smile; this is a charm that even they cannot claim. It is the prerogative of man; it is the color which love wears, and cheerfulness and joy— these three. *—H. W. Beecher.*

HELPFULNESS

It is not possible, ordinarily, to change the hard conditions of those who are in life's stress; but it is possible to give them brotherly sympathy and encouragement. The cup was not taken away from Jesus, but an angel from heaven appeared and strengthened Him. No other ministry which human love can render is so angel-like as that of him who gives cheer.   —*J. R. Miller.*

It is not how many bonds you have in a bank vault, or how much plate on your sideboard that God looks to see, but how many lives have been brightened and how many sorrows have been healed by the gifts of your love. —*H. C. Potter.*

The worst days of darkness through which I have ever passed have been greatly alleviated by throwing myself with all my energy into some work relating to others.   —*Garfield.*

> Loving words will cost but little
> Journeying up the hill of life;
> But they make the weak and weary
> Stronger, braver, for the strife.

Do you count them only trifles?
What to earth are sun and rain?
Never was a kind word wasted;
Never was one said in vain.
—*Anonymous.*

Without the wisdom of the learned, the clown could not be governed; without the labor of the clown, the learned could not be fed.
—*"Wisdom of the Chinese."*

There is a destiny that makes us brothers;
None goes his way alone;
All that we send into the lives of others
Comes back into our own.
—*Edwin Markham.*

I SHALL NOT PASS AGAIN THIS WAY

The bread that bringeth strength I want to give;
The water pure that bids the thirsty live.
I want to help the fainting, day by day.
I'm sure I shall not pass again this way.

I want to give the oil of joy for tears,
The faith to conquer crowding doubts and fears;
Beauty for ashes may I give alway.
I'm sure I shall not pass again this way.

I want to give good measure running o'er,
And into angry hearts I want to pour
The answer soft that turneth wrath away.
I'm sure I shall not pass again this way.

I want to give to others hope and faith;
I want to do all that the Master saith;
I want to do aright from day to day.
I'm sure I shall not pass again this way.

—Anonymous.

It's everybody's business
    In this old world of ours,
To pull up all the weeds we find
    To make room for the flowers,
So that every little garden
    No matter where it lies
Will look like the one God made
    And called it Paradise.

—Anonymous.

A DAY WELL SPENT

If you sit down at set of sun
And count the deeds that you have done,
And, counting, find
One self-denying act, one word

That eased the heart of him that heard;
One glance most kind
Which felt like sunshine where it went,
Then you may count that day well spent.

But if through all the livelong day
You've eased no heart by yea or nay,
If through it all you've nothing done
That you can trace;
That brought the sunshine to one face;
No act most small that helped
Some soul and nothing cost;
Then count that day as worse than lost.

—*Anonymous.*

FOR THE GOOD OF ALL

Let every man and woman be industrious, prudent and economical in their acts and feelings, and while gathering to themselves, let each one strive to identify his or her interests with the interests of the community, with those of their neighbor and neighborhood, let them seek their happiness and welfare in that of all, and we will be blessed and prospered.

—*Brigham Young.*

We cannot all be heroes,
    And thrill a hemisphere
With some great, daring venture,
    Some deed that mocks at fear;
But we can fill a lifetime
    With kindly acts and true;
There's always noble service
    For noble souls to do.

—*C. A. Mason.*

HOME AND FAMILY

If God hath made this world so fair
    Where sin and death abound,
How beautiful beyond compare
    Will paradise be found!

—*James Montgomery.*

So long as there are homes to which men turn
    at close of day—
So long as there are homes where children are;
    where women stay—
If love and loyalty and faith be found
    across those sills—
A stricken nation can recover from
    its gravest ills.

—*Grace Noll Crowell.*

We need not power nor splendor,
　Wide hall nor lordly dome;
The good, the true, the tender—
　These form the wealth of home.
　　　　　　　—*Anonymous.*

What makes a home? 'Tis where the weary come
And lay their burdens down, assured of rest.
Where we learn to know our dearest best;
Where children play, blessing and blest—
Though walls of coarsest clay enwrap the nest.
　　　　　　　—*Fanny S. Reeder.*

We have careful thoughts for the stranger,
And smiles for the sometime guest,
　But oft for "our own"
　The bitter tone
Though we love "our own" the best.
Ah, lips with the curve impatient!
Ah, brow with that look of scorn!
　'Twere a cruel fate
　Were the night too late
To undo the work of the morn.
　　　　　　　—*Margaret Sangster.*

THOUGHTS OF HOME

The pleasant converse of the fireside, the simple songs of the home, the words of encouragement as I bend over my school tasks, the kiss as I lie down to rest, the patient bearing with the freaks of my restless nature, the gentle counsels mingled with reproofs and approval, the sympathy that meets and assuages every sorrow and sweetens every little success—all these return to me amid the responsibilities which press upon me now, and I feel as if I had once lived in heaven and, straying, had lost my way.   —*J. G. Holland.*

Happy are the families where the government of parents is the reign of affection, and the obedience of the children is the submission of love.   —*Anonymous.*

There is no happiness, there is no misery, like that growing out of the dispositions which consecrate or desecrate a home.   —*E. H. Chapin.*

CHILDREN WITHOUT CHASTISEMENT

Soft-hearted mothers rear soft-hearted children. They hurt them for life because they are afraid of hurting them while they are young. Coddle your children, and they will turn out noodles. You may sugar a child till every body is sick of it. Boys' jackets need a little dusting every now and then, and girls' dresses are all the better for occasional trimming. Children without chastisement are fields without plowing. The very best colts want breaking in. Not that we like severity. Cruel mothers are not mothers, and those who are always flogging and fault-finding ought to be flogged themselves. There is reason in all things, as the madman said when he cut off his nose.

—*Spurgeon.*

IF JESUS CAME TO YOUR HOUSE

If Jesus came to your house to spend a day or two—
If He came unexpectedly, I wonder what you'd do.
Oh, I know you'd give your nicest room to such an honored Guest,
And all the food you'd serve to Him would be the very best,
And you would keep assuring Him you're glad to have Him there—

That serving Him in your home is joy beyond
compare.

But—when you saw Him coming would you meet
Him at the door

With arms outstretched in welcome to your
heav'nly Visitor?

Or would you have to change your clothes before
you let Him in,

Or hide some magazines and put the Bible where
they'd been?

Would you turn off the radio and hope He hadn't
heard,

And wish you hadn't uttered that last, loud, hasty
word?

Would you hide your worldly music and put some
hymn books out?

Could you let Jesus walk right in, or would you
rush about?

And I wonder—if the Savior spent a day or two
with you,

Would you go right on doing the things you
always do?

Would you go right on saying the things you
always say?

Would life for you continue as it does from day
to day?

Would your family conversation keep up its usual
   pace,
And would you find it hard each meal to say a
   table grace?
Would you sing the songs you always sing and
   read the books you read,
And let Him know the things on which your mind
   and spirit feed?
Would you take Jesus with you everywhere you
   planned to go,
Or would you, maybe, change your plans for just
   a day or so.
Would you be glad to have Him meet your very
   closest friends,
Or would you hope they'd stay away until His
   visit ends?
Would you be glad to have Him stay forever on
   and on,
Or would you sigh with great relief when He at
   last was gone?
It might be interesting to know the things that
   you would do,
If Jesus came in person to spend some time with
   you.

—Anonymous.

HUMILITY

The true way to be humble is not to stoop till you are smaller than yourself, but to stand at your real height against some higher nature that shall show you what the real smallness of your greatness is.   —*Phillips Brooks.*

I give unto men weakness that they may be humble; and my grace is sufficient for all men that humble themselves before me;
                    —*Ether* 12:27.

Come unto me, all ye that labor and are heavy laden, and I will give you rest.

Take my yoke upon you, and learn of me; for I am meek and lowly in heart; and ye shall find rest unto your souls.

For my yoke is easy, and my burden is light.
                    —*Matt.* 11:28-30.

JUSTICE—JUDGMENT

For he who is not able to abide the law of a celestial kingdom cannot abide a celestial glory.

And he who cannot abide the law of a terrestrial kingdom cannot abide a terrestrial glory.

And he who cannot abide the law of a telestial kingdom cannot abide a telestial glory; therefore he is not meet for a kingdom of glory. Therefore he must abide a kingdom which is not a kingdom of glory.   —*D. & C.* 88:22-24.

Correct yourselves on the same principle that you correct others, and excuse others on the same principle that you excuse yourselves.

—*"Wisdom of the Chinese."*

Behold, I say unto you that ye would be more miserable to dwell with a holy and just God, under a consciousness of your filthiness before him, than ye would to dwell with the damned souls in hell.   —*Mormon* 9:4.

Mercy claimeth the penitent, and mercy cometh because of the atonement; and the atonement bringeth to pass the resurrection of the dead; and the resurrection of the dead bringeth back men into the presence of God; thus they are restored into his presence, to be judged according to their works, according to the law and justice. For behold, justice exerciseth all his demands, and also mercy claimeth all which is her own; and thus, none but the truly penitent are saved.

—*Alma* 42:23, 24, *B. of M.*

KINDNESS

If you were busy being kind,
Before you knew it, you would find
You'd soon forget to think 'twas true
That someone was unkind to you.

If you were busy being glad
And cheering people who were sad,
Although your heart might ache a bit
You'd soon forget to notice it.

If you were busy being true
To what you know you ought to do,
You'd be so busy you'd forget
The blunders of the folks you've met.

—*Anonymous.*

Better do a kindness near home than go far to
burn incense.

To save one life is better than to build a
seven-story pagoda.

—*"Wisdom of the Chinese."*

O, what a little thing can turn
A heavy heart from sighs to song!
A smile can make the world less stern,

A word can cause the soul to burn
With glow of heaven, all night long.
                        —*Anonymous.*

There is a destiny that makes us brothers;
None goes his way alone;
All that we send into the lives of others
Comes back into our own.
                        —*Edwin Markham.*

I met a little maid
   A rosy burden bearing;
"Is he not heavy?" I said
   As past me she was hurrying.
She looked at me with grave, sweet eyes,
   This fragile little mother,
And answered in swift surprise:
   "Oh, no Sir. He's my brother."
                        —*Anonymous.*

MERCY

The quality of mercy is not strained;
It droppeth as the gentle rain from heaven
Upon the place beneath: it is twice blest—
It blesseth him that gives and him that takes;

'Tis mightiest in the mightiest; it becomes
The throned monarch better than his crown;
His sceptre shows the force of temporal power,
The attribute to awe and majesty,
Wherein doth sit the dread and fear of kings;
But mercy is above this sceptred sway—
It is enthroned in the hearts of kings,
It is an attribute of God himself;
And earthly power doth then show likest God's,
When mercy seasons justice.

—Shakespeare.
From "Merchant of Venice."

LIFE IS TOO SHORT

Life is too short for words that hurt;
For subtle thrusts and for phrases curt;
For motives unkind and for sharp retort—
For any of these, life is too short.

—Lucile Veneklasen.

LET SOMETHING GOOD BE SAID

When over the fair frame of friend or foe
    The shadow of disgrace shall fall, instead
Of words of blame, or proof of thus and so,
    Let something good be said.

Forget not that no fellow-being yet
  May fall so low but love may lift his head;
Even the cheek of shame with tears is wet,
  If something good be said.

And so I charge ye, by the thorny crown,
  And by the cross on which the Savior bled,
And by your own soul's hope of fair renown,
  Let something good be said!

—James Whitcomb Riley.

LIFE AND LIVING

Great results cannot be achieved at once, and we must be satisfied to advance in life as we walk —step by step. *—Samuel Smiles.*

If you can sit at set of sun
And count the deeds that you have done
  And counting find
One self-denying act, one word
That eased the heart of him that heard—
  One glance most kind,
Which fell like sunshine where he went,
Then you may count that day well spent.

—Robert Browning.

Be good; get good, and do good. Do all the good you can, to all the people you can, in all the ways you can, as often as ever you can, as long as you can.   —*Charles H. Spurgeon.*

If we abide by the principles taught in the Bible, our country will go on prospering and to prosper, but if we and our posterity neglect its instruction and authority, no man can tell how sudden a catastrophe may overwhelm us and bury our glory in profound obscurity.

—*Daniel Webster.*

WHAT I LIVE FOR

I live for those who love me,
  For those I know are true,
For the heaven that smiles above me,
  And awaits my spirit too,
For all human ties that bind me,
  For the task my God assigned me,
For the bright hopes yet to find me,
  And the good that I can do.

I live to hail that season
  By gifted ones foretold,

When men shall live by reason,
  And not alone for gold,
When, man to man united
  And every wrong thing righted,
The whole world shall be lighted
  As Eden was of old.

I live for those who love me,
  For those who know me true,
For the heaven that smiles above me
  And awaits my spirit too,
For the cause that lacks assistance,
  For the wrong that needs resistance,
For the future in the distance,
  And the good that I can do.

—*George L. Banks.*

Dost thou love life? Then do not squander time, for that is the stuff life is made of.

—*Franklin.*

He who can not forgive others breaks the bridge over which he must pass himself.

—*George Herbert.*

Man cannot reach perfection in a hundred years, but he can fall in a day with time to spare.

—*"Wisdom of the Chinese."*

TIME AND ETERNITY

The flowers fade, the heart withers, man grows old and dies, the world lies down in the sepulcher of ages; but time writes no wrinkles on the brow of eternity.   —*Bishop Heber.*

A good, practical education, including a good trade, is a better outfit for a youth than a grand estate with the drawback of an empty mind. Many parents have slaved and pinched to leave their children rich, when half the sum thus lavished would have profited them far more had it been devoted to the cultivation of their minds, the enlargement of their capacity to think, observe and work. The one structure that no neighborhood can afford to do without is the school-house.

—*Horace Greeley.*

To mourn a mischief that is past and gone
Is the best way to bring a fresh mischief on.
—*William Shakespeare.*

Look well to this day!
For it is life; the very life of life.
In its brief course lie all the verities
　　And realities of your existence.

The bliss of growth, the glory of action,
The splendor of beauty;
For yesterday is only a dream,
Tomorrow is only a vision;
But today, well lived, makes of every yesterday
A dream of happiness and of every tomorrow
  A vision of hope.
Look well, therefore, to this day.
                                        —Anonymous.

. . . let virtue garnish thy thoughts unceasingly; then shall thy confidence wax strong in the presence of God; and the doctrine of the priesthood shall distil upon thy soul as the dews from heaven.

The Holy Ghost shall be thy constant companion, and thy scepter an unchanging scepter of righteousness and truth; and thy dominion shall be an everlasting dominion, and without compulsory means it shall flow unto thee forever and ever.   *—D. & C.* 121:45-46.

TOMORROW

High hopes that burned like stars sublime
  Go down the heavens of freedom,
And true hearts perish in the time
  We bitterliest need them.

But never sit we down and say:
  "There's nothing left but sorrow."
We walk the wilderness today—
  The Promised Land tomorrow.

Then youth, flame earnest, still aspire
  With energies immortal;
To many a haven of desire
  Your yearning opes a portal.
And though age wearies by the way,
  And hearts break in the furrow,
We sow the golden grain today—
  The harvest comes tomorrow.

                —*Gerald Massey.*

WE LIVE IN DEEDS

We live in deeds, not years; in thoughts, not
breaths; in feelings, not in figures on a dial. We
should count time by heart-throbs. He most lives
who thinks most, feels the noblest, acts the best.
                —*J. P. Bailey.*

A PSALM OF LIFE

Tell me not, in mournful numbers,
  "Life is but an empty dream!"
For the soul is dead that slumbers,
  And things are not what they seem.

Life is real! Life is earnest!
  And the grave is not its goal;
"Dust thou art, to dust returnest,"
  Was not spoken of the soul.

Not enjoyment, and not sorrow,
  Is our destined end or way;
But to act that each to-morrow
  Finds us farther than to-day.

Art is long, and time is fleeting,
  And our hearts, though stout and brave,
Still, like muffled drums, are beating
  Funeral marches to the grave.

In the world's broad field of battle,
  In the bivouac of life,
Be not like dumb, driven cattle!
  Be a hero in the strife!

Trust no future, howe'er pleasant!
  Let the dead past bury its dead!
Act, act in the living present!
  Heart within, and God o'erhead!

Lives of great men all remind us
  We can make our lives sublime,
And, departing, leave behind us
  Footprints on the sands of time;

Footprints, that perhaps another,
  Sailing o'er life's solemn main,
A forlorn and shipwrecked brother,
  Seeing, shall take heart again.

Let us, then, be up and doing,
  With a heart for any fate;
Still achieving, still pursuing,
  Learn to labor and to wait.
                    —*Henry W. Longfellow.*

I know not when I go or where
  From this familiar scene;
But He is here and He is there,
  And all the way between;
And when I leave this life, I know,
  For that vast and dim unknown,
Though late I stay, or soon I go,
  I shall not go alone.
                    —*Anonymous.*

Lord, give me not just words to say,
  Though I need right words too;
But strength to live in such a way
  My life will make my words come true.
                    —*Anonymous.*

NOT IN VAIN

If I can stop one heart from breaking,
I shall not live in vain:
If I can ease one life the aching,
Or cool one pain,
Or help one fainting robin
Unto his nest again,
I shall not live in vain.

—Emily Dickinson.

EVERY DAY THE BEST

One of the illusions is that the present hour is not the critical, decisive hour. Write it on your heart that every day is the best day in the year.

—Emerson.

THE LOOM OF LIFE

All day, all night, I can hear the jar
Of the loom of life; and near and far
It thrills with its deep and muffled sound,
As the tireless wheels go always around.

Busily, ceaselessly goes the loom
In the light of day and the midnight's gloom.
The wheels are turning early and late,
And the woof is wound in the warp of fate.

Click, clack! There's a thread of love wove in.
Click, clack! And another of wrong and sin.
What a checkered thing will this life be
When we see it unrolled in eternity!

Time, with a face like mystery
And hands as busy as hands can be,
Sits at the loom with its warp outspread,
To catch in its meshes each glancing thread.

When shall this wonderful web be done?
In a thousand years, perhaps—or one—
Or tomorrow. Who knoweth? Not you nor I.
But the wheels turn on, and the shuttles fly.

Ah, sad-eyed weaver! The years are slow,
But each one is nearer the end, I know;
And some day the last thread shall be woven in—
God grant it be love instead of sin!

                                        —*Anonymous.*

HOW DID YOU DIE?

———

Did you tackle the trouble that came your way
  With a resolute heart and cheerful?
Or hide your face from the light of day
  With a craven soul and fearful?
Oh, a trouble's a ton, or a trouble's an ounce,
  Or a trouble is what you make it.
And it isn't the fact that you're hurt that counts,
  But only how did you take it?

You are beaten to earth? Well, well, what's that?
  Come up with a smiling face.
It's nothing against you to fall down flat,
  But to lie there—that's disgrace.
The harder you're thrown, why the higher you
    bounce;
  Be proud of your blackened eye!
It isn't the fact that you're licked that counts;
  It's how did you fight and why?

And though you be done to death, what then?
  If you battled the best you could;
If you played your part in the world of men,
  Why, the Critic will call it good.

Death comes with a crawl, or comes with a pounce,
  And whether he's slow or spry,
It isn't the fact that you're dead that counts,
  But only, how did you die?
                              —*Anonymous.*

JOHN QUINCY ADAM'S HOUSE

———

It has been said that when walking down the street one day the ex-President was addressed by a friend who said: "Mr. Adams, how are you?" The old gentleman pleasantly replied: "Thank you, sir! John Quincy Adams himself is well, sir, quite well. I thank you. But the house in which he lives at present is becoming dilapidated. It is tottering upon its foundations. Time and the seasons have nearly destroyed it. Its roof is pretty well wornout. Its walls are much shattered, and it trembles with every wind. The old tenement is becoming almost uninhabitable, and I think John Quincy Adams will have to move out of it soon; but he, himself, is quite well, sir, quite well."
                              —*Anonymous.*

ENDURING VALUES

There are some old things we cannot dispense with, and among these are God's word and truth, and those religious influences by which He brings the heart of man into subjection to moral law. Do not be ashamed to confess yourselves Christians. To me, one all-important thing is that we should have a freer flow of conversation relating to nature, God and eternity. I have always had a sort of compassion for those who think they are wiser than the Creator. There is a God, and if a God, then a governor. He has not created us and flung us out to be the mere sport of chance and time. But I will not dwell upon the relation of science to religion. I will only add that he is as cruel who attempts to scorn away and overthrow religion as he who knocks the crutches from beneath a lame man. In the observances of the laws of God and in the promise of the Gospel of Jesus Christ there is the best guarantee of peace upon earth and the only hope of eternal life.

—*Benjamin Harrison.*

A WAY TO HEALTH

Positive teachings—eat meat very sparingly, eat fresh fruit liberally, eat fresh and cooked vegetables regularly, eat grains in bread or porridge daily, drink water, fruit juices, grain extracts or milk in abundance, sleep regularly from early evening to early morning, labor regularly and steadily with body and mind, secure a correct mental attitude— have faith, hope and charity, and seek and practice the truths of religion.

Negative teachings—drink no alcoholic beverages. Use no tobacco, drink no tea or coffee and avoid refined foods.

Rewards of observance—health of body, mental efficiency, immunity from disease and spiritual joy and understanding.   —*Anonymous.*

IT'S THE LIFE YOU ARE LIVING THAT COUNTS

You may sing loud the praises of God unto man,
  But a truth here, my friend, I announce:
It's not all in the singing or preaching the word,
  It's the life you are living that counts.

You may give very freely of silver or gold,
  And frequently utter long prayers;
But a man shall be known by his every-day walk,
  And be judged by the fruit that he bears.

                      —Anonymous.

POEM OF LIFE

At times we've thought what is the use
To brave the world and its abuse?
Trouble and sorrow seem everywhere
Surely 'tis more than we can bear.

But then a still, small voice would say,
There's joy for you if you'll but pay.
Should roses grow without a thorn?
To unearned ease are mortals born?

The sweetest flowers ofttimes are found
Amid the thorns in roughened ground.
And richest joys you'll find are those
Which spring from work and not repose.

                      —Hamblen.

We are very apt to measure ourselves by our aspiration instead of our performance. But in truth the conduct of our lives is the only proof of the sincerity of our hearts.   *—Anonymous.*

LIVE FOR SOMETHING

Live for something, have a purpose,
  And that purpose keep in view;
Drifting like a helmless vessel,
  Thou canst ne'er to life be true.
Half the wrecks that strew life's ocean,
  If some star had been their guide,
Might have now been riding safely,
  But they drifted with the tide.

Live for something, and live earnest,
  Though the work may humble be,
By the world of men unnoticed,
  Known alone to God and thee.
Every act has priceless value
  To the architect of fate;
'Tis the spirit of thy doing
  That alone will make it great.

Live for something—God and angels
  Are thy watchers in the strife,
And above the smoke and conflict
  Gleams the victor's crown of life.
Live for something; God has given
  Freely of his stores divine;
Richest gifts of earth and heaven,
  If thou willst, may be thine.
                    —*Robert Whitaker*.

We go through life as some tourists go through Europe—so anxious to see the next sight, the next cathedral, the next picture, the next mountain peak, that we never stop to fill our sense with the beauty of the present one.   —*Minot J. Savage.*

THE LIFE THAT COUNTS

The life that counts must toil and fight;
Must hate the wrong and love the right;
Must stand for truth, by day, by night—
This is the life that counts.

The life that counts must helpful be;
The cares and needs of others see;
Must seek the slaves of sin to free—
This is the life that counts.

—*Anonymous.*

ADVICE ABOUT SLANDER

Your blameless life will be your best defense, and those who have seen it will not allow you to be condemned so readily as your slanderers expect. Only abstain from fighting your own battles, and in nine cases out of ten your accusers will gain nothing by their malevolence but chagrin for themselves and contempt from others. To prosecute the slanderer is very seldom wise.   —*Spurgeon.*

SMOOTHING THE ROAD

———

A man was limping along a country road. "This road is too rough," he complained to the man with him. "My foot aches so much, I can hardly walk."

"The road's not too rough for me," his friend replied. "But if you want to, we'll stop and rest."

"Let's do," agreed the first man. The men sat down and the one man removed his shoe. As he did, a small pebble rolled out and fell to the ground.

The pebble was at fault, not the road. Isn't it true that a lot of us blame the road when it's really just a pebble in our shoe. We think the whole road is rough. And, looking back over something that seemed extremely hard and rough, we wonder how we got through it so easily. The mental pebbles we put in our shoes make the job hard—not the job itself. Once we get rid of the mental obstacle, our whole attitude is different.

Next time the road looks rough to you, see if it isn't just a pebble that got between you and the road.   —*"Mutual Moments."*

LIGHT AND LEARNING

And that which doth not edify is not of God, and is darkness.

That which is of God is light; and he that receiveth light, and continueth in God, receiveth more light; and that light groweth brighter and brighter until the perfect day.

—*D. & C.* 50:23-24.

LIVING IN THE LIGHT

Look toward the light. That is the way we should learn to live. If we look ever toward the light, the light will enter into us and fill us with its own radiance.

Let us walk in the light while we have the light, and we shall become the children of light. Then no darkness can overtake us, or quench the light that shines in us. Then shall we be able to brighten other lives in their sorrow.

Nothing makes life so sweet in old age as the memory of right and good things done along the years. Such gathering in the summer days of life will make the winter cheerful and bright, even with storm and darkness outside.

Take into your heart every day some cheering word of God. Listen to some heavenly song of hope and joy. Let your eye dwell on some beautiful vision of divine love. Thus your very soul will become a fountain of light and joy; and gladness will become more and more the dominant mood of your life.   —*Dr. J. R. Miller.*

Evil and sin thrive best under cover of darkness.

God, our Heavenly Father, is a God of light. From Him radiates the light that lights the world.

In the process of creation God said: "Let there be light." There was light and it was good.

When God spoke to Moses it seemed to him as if from a bush that was on fire but not consumed.

When messengers have come from heaven to men on earth, they have appeared as in a blaze of light.

Behold, I am the light and life of the world.
—*D.C.* 12:9.

I am the true light that lighteth every man that cometh into the world.   —*D.C.* 93:2.

Behold, I am Jesus Christ the Son of God. I am the same that came unto mine own, and mine own received me not. I am the light that shineth in darkness, and the darkness comprehendeth it not. —D.C. 6:21.

That which doth not edify is not of God, and is darkness. That which is of God is light, and he that receiveth light, and continueth in God, receiveth more light and that light groweth brighter and brighter until the perfect day.

—D.C. 50:23, 24.

If your eye be single to my glory, your whole bodies shall be filled with light, and there shall be no darkness in you and that body which is filled with light comprehendeth all things.

—D.C. 88:67.

The Spirit of truth is of God. I am the Spirit of truth, and John bore record of me, saying; He received a fulness of truth, yea, even of all truth;

And no man receiveth a fulness unless he keepeth his commandments.

He that keepeth his commandments receiveth truth and light, until he is glorified in truth and knoweth all things.

And every man whose spirit receiveth not the light is under condemnation.

The glory of God is intelligence, or, in other words, light and truth.   —*D.C.* 93:26-36.

* * *

O that cunning plan of the evil one! O the vainness, and the frailties, and the foolishness of men! When they are learned they think they are wise, and they hearken not unto the counsel of God, for they set it aside, supposing they know of themselves, wherefore, their wisdom is foolishness and it profiteth them not. And they shall perish.

But to be learned is good if they hearken unto the counsels of God.   —*II Ne.* 9:28-29.

MOTHER

What would you take for that soft little head
  Pressed close to your face at time of bed;
For that white, dimpled hand in your own held
    tight,
  And the dear little eyelids kissed down for the
    night?
        What would you take?

What would you take for that smile in the morn,
  Those bright, dancing eyes and the face they
    adorn;
For the sweet little voice that you hear all day
  Laughing and cooing—yet nothing to say?
        What would you take?

What would you take for those pink little feet,
  Those chubby round cheeks, and that mouth so
    sweet;
For the wee tiny fingers and little soft toes,
  The wrinkly little neck and that funny little
    nose?
        What would you take?
            —*Good Housekeeping.*

BUT ONLY ONE MOTHER

———

Most of all the other beautiful things in life
come by twos and threes, by dozens and hundreds.
Plenty of roses, stars, sunsets, rainbows, brothers
and sisters, aunts and cousins, but only one
mother in the whole world.
            —*Kate Douglas Wiggin.*

OPPORTUNITY

Out of eternity this new day is born;
Into eternity at night will return.
Behold it aforetime, no eye ever did;
So soon it forever from all eyes is hid.
So here hath been dawning another blue day;
Think, wilt thou let it slip useless away?
                              —*Thomas Carlyle.*

EACH DAY HAS ITS OPPORTUNITY

All the days seem alike as they come to us, but each day comes with its own opportunities, its own calls to duty, its own privileges—holding out hands offering us radiant gifts. The day passes and never comes again. Other days as bright may come, but that day never comes a second time. If we do not take just then the gifts it offers, we shall never have another chance to get them, and shall always be poorer for what we have missed.

                              —*Dr. J. R. Miller.*

They who know how to employ opportunities will often find that they can create them, and what we can achieve depends less on the amount of time we possess than on the use we make of our time.   —*J. S. Mill.*

PATRIOTISM

AMERICA FOR ME

'Tis fine to see the Old World, and travel up and
down
Among the famous palaces and cities of renown,
To admire the crumbly castles and the statues of
the kings—
But now I think I've had enough of antiquated
things.

I know that Europe's wonderful, yet something
seems to lack:
The past is too much with her, and the people
looking back.
But the glory of the present is to make the future
free—
We love our land for what she is and what she is
to be.

So it's home again, and home again, America for
me!
My heart is turning home again, and there I long
to be,
In the land of youth and freedom beyond the
ocean bars,
Where the air is full of sunlight and the flag is
full of stars.   —*Henry Van Dyke.*

MY NATIVE LAND

———

Breathes there a man with soul so dead,
Who never to himself hath said:
   "This is my own, my native land"?
Whose heart hath ne'er within him burned
As home his footsteps he hath turned,
   From wandering on a foreign strand?
If such there breathe, go, mark him well;
For him no minstrel raptures swell!
High though his titles, proud his name,
Boundless his wealth as wish can claim—
Despite those titles, power and pelf,
The wretch concentered all in self,
Living, shall forfeit fair renown,
And doubly dying, shall go down
To the vile dust, from whence he sprung,
Unwept, unhonored and unsung.

          —*Sir Walter Scott.*

America is only another name for opportunity.
          —*Emerson.*

PEACE—PEACEMAKERS

BLESSED ARE THE PEACEMAKERS

There are causes enough to separate people and to produce frictions and alienations. Let us not add to the world's bitterness and grief by ever encouraging strife, or putting a single coal on the fire of anger. Rather let us try to heal the little rifts we find in people's friendships. The unkind thoughts we find in another's mind, let us try to change to kindly thoughts, continually seeking to promote peace between man and man, to keep people from drifting apart, and to draw friends and neighbors closer together in love.

—*Dr. J. R. Miller.*

For verily, verily I say unto you, he that hath the spirit of contention is not of me, but is of the devil, who is the father of contention, and he stirreth up the hearts of men to contend with anger, one with another.   —*III Nephi* 11:29.

Peace I leave with you, my peace I give unto you; not as the world giveth, give I unto you. Let not your heart be troubled, neither let it be afraid.   —*John* 14:27.

PRAYER

MY TODAY

I have no other day than this;
O Father, grant I shall not miss
The service sweet of doing good,
And living truly as I should.

O Father, in this day that's mine
Let all thy sweetness through me shine;
Let all my ways acknowledge thee,
May Christ be manifest in me.

Oh! let me be thy voice to speak
The truth to those who vainly seek;
And through me let thy love o'erflow
To all the world that needs it so.

Oh! let today be this for me,
A day of glorifying thee.
'Tis all the day that my soul knows;
'Tis from today tomorrow grows.

So, for today, this is my prayer,
Tomorrow, Lord, is in thy care.

—Mabel F. Ricard.

Prayer will make a man cease from sin, or sin
will entice a man to cease from prayer.

—*Bunyan.*

Make my mortal dreams come true,
With the work I fain would do;
Clothe with life the weak intent,
Let me be the thing I meant;
Let me find in Thy employ,
Peace that dearer is than joy.

—*Whittier.*

GOD'S BETTER ANSWER

God many times answers our prayers not by
bringing down his will to ours, but lifting us up
to himself. We grow strong, so as to need no
longer cry for relief. We can bear the heavy load
without asking to have it lightened. We can keep
the sorrow now and endure it. We can go on in
quiet peace without the new blessing which we
thought so necessary. We have not been saved
from the battle we shrank so from entering, but
we have sought and have gained the victory. Is
not victoriousness in conflict better than being

freed from the struggle? Is not peace in the midst of the storm and the strife better than to be lifted altogether over the strife?

—Dr. J. R. Miller.

MY PRAYER

More holiness give me, more strivings within;
More patience in suff'ring, more sorrow for sin;
More faith in my Savior, more sense of His care;
More joy in His service, more purpose in prayer.

More gratitude give me, more trust in the Lord;
More pride in His glory, more hope in His word;
More tears for His sorrows, more pain at His grief;
More meekness in trial, more praise for relief.

More purity give me, more strength to o'er-come;
More freedom from earth-stains, more longings
   for home;
More fit for the kingdom, more used would I be;
More blessed and holy, more Savior *like Thee.*

—P. P. Bliss.

Guide me, O Lord, in all the changes and varieties of this world; that in all things that shall happen, I may have an evenness and tran-

quility of spirit; that my soul may be wholly re-
signed to thy divine will and pleasure.

—*Jeremy Taylor.*

Yea, and I also exhort you, my brethren, that ye
be watchful unto prayer continually, that ye may
not be led away by the temptation of the devil,
that he may not overpower you, that ye may not
become his subjects at the last day; for behold, he
rewardeth you no good thing.   —*Alma* 35:39.

PRAYER

My life has taught me day by day
That it availeth much to pray.

I do not stop to reason out
    The why and how. I do not care,
Since I know this, that when I doubt,
    Life seems a blackness of despair,
The world a tomb; and when I trust,
Sweet blossoms spring up in the dust.

Since I know in the darkest hour,
    If I lift up my soul in prayer,
Some sympathetic, loving Power
    Sends hope and comfort to me there.
Since balm is sent to ease my pain,
What need to argue or explain?

Prayer has a sweet refining grace,
　　It educates the soul and heart.
It lends a luster to the face,
　　And by its elevating art
It gives the mind an inner sight
That brings it near the Infinite.

From our gross selves it helps us rise
　　To something, which we yet may be,
And so I ask not to be wise,
　　If thus my faith is lost to me—
Faith that with angel's voice and touch,
Says "Pray, for prayer availeth much."

　　　　　　　—*Ella Wheeler Wilcox.*

THIS IS MY PRAYER

Give me a pulsing heart to feel
The need of other hearts, and kneel
With them when lonely shadows steal
　　Across the way.

Give me a vibrant hand and strong
To right a weaker brother's wrong,
Or smooth some tangled place along
　　His onward way.

Give me a spirit swift to greet,
And lay life's incense at the feet
Of every soul I chance to meet
    Upon the way.

Give me to feel with kindness rare,
Give me to act with courage fair,
Give me to bless. This is my prayer
    Along the way.
                  —Anonymous.

PROCRASTINATION

BEHIND TIME

The best-laid plans, the most important affairs, the fortunes of individuals, the weal of nations, honor, life itself, are daily sacrificed because somebody is "behind time." There are men who always fail in whatever they undertake simply because they are "behind time." There are others who put off reformation year by year, till death seizes them; and they perish unrepentant, because for ever "behind time." Five minutes in a crisis is worth years. It is but a little period, yet it has often saved a fortune or redeemed a people. If there is one virtue that should be cultivated more than another by him who would succeed in life, it is punctuality; if there is one error that should be avoided, it is being "behind time."

—*Freeman Hunt.*

AMULEK WARNS AGAINST PROCRASTINATION

———

For behold, this life is the time for men to prepare to meet God; yea, behold the day of this life is the day for men to perform their labors.

And now, as I said unto you before, as ye have had so many witnesses, therefore, I beseech of you that ye do not procrastinate the day of your repentance until the end; for after this day of life, which is given us to prepare for eternity, behold, if we do not improve our time while in this life, then cometh the night of darkness wherein there can be no labor performed.

Ye cannot say, when ye are brought to that awful crisis, that I will repent, that I will return to my God. Nay, ye cannot say this; for that same spirit which doth possess your bodies at the time that ye go out of this life, that same spirit will have power to possess your body in that eternal world.

For behold, if ye have procrastinated the day of your repentance even until death, behold, ye have become subjected to the spirit of the devil, and he doth seal you his. —*Alma* 34:32-35.

PROVERBS AND PSALMS

Happy is the man that findeth wisdom, and the man that getteth understanding:

For the merchandise of it is better than the merchandise of silver, and the gain thereof than fine gold.

She is more precious than rubies: and all the things thou canst desire are not to be compared unto her.

Length of days is in her right hand; and in her left hand riches and honour.

Her ways are ways of pleasantness, and all her paths are peace.

She is a tree of life to them that lay hold upon her; and happy is every one that retaineth her.

The Lord by wisdom hath founded the earth; by understanding hath he established the heavens.

By his knowledge the depths are broken up, and the clouds drop down the dew.

My son, let not them depart from thine eyes; keep sound wisdom and discretion.

—Proverbs 3:13-21.

The fear of the Lord is the beginning of knowledge; but fools despise wisdom and instruction.   *—Proverbs* 1:7.

Trust in the Lord with all thine heart; and lean not unto thine own understanding.

—Proverbs 3:5.

Wisdom is the principal thing; therefore get wisdom; and with all thy getting get understanding.   *—Proverbs* 4:7.

These six things doth the Lord hate: yea, seven are an abomination unto him:

The proud look, a lying tongue, and hands that shed innocent blood, an heart that deviseth wicked imaginations, feet that be swift in running to mischief, a false witness that speaketh lies, and he that soweth discord among brethren.

—Proverbs 6:16-19.

A false balance is abomination to the Lord; but a just weight is his delight.   —*Proverbs* 11:1.

There is a way which seemeth right unto a man, but the end thereof are the ways of death.
—*Proverbs* 14:12.

He that despiseth his neighbor sinneth; but he that hath mercy on the poor, happy is he.
—*Proverbs* 14:21.

He that is slow to wrath is of great understanding; but he that is hasty of spirit exalteth folly.
—*Proverbs* 14:29.

Righteousness exalteth a nation; but sin is a reproach to any people.   —*Proverbs* 14:34.

A soft answer turneth away wrath; but grievous words stireth up anger.   —*Proverbs* 15:1.

A fool despiseth his father's instruction; but he that regardeth reproof is prudent.
—*Proverbs* 15:5.

The heart of him that hath understanding seeketh knowledge; but the mouth of fools feedeth on foolishness.   —*Proverbs* 15:14.

Better is little with the fear of the Lord than great treasure and trouble therewith.

—Proverbs 15:16.

He that is slow to anger is better than the mighty; and he that ruleth his spirit than he that taketh a city.   *—Proverbs* 16:32.

A merry heart doeth good like a medicine; but a broken spirit drieth the bones.

—Proverbs 17:22.

Wine is a mocker, strong drink is raging; and whosoever is deceived thereby is not wise.

—Proverbs 20:1.

To do justice and judgment is more acceptable to the Lord than sacrifice.   *—Proverbs* 21:3.

A good name is rather to be chosen than great riches, and loving favor rather than silver and gold.   *—Proverbs* 22:1.

Seest thou a man diligent in his business? he shall stand before kings; he shall not stand before mean men.   *—Proverbs* 22:29.

Where no wood is, there the fire goeth out; so where there is no talebearer, the strife ceaseth.

—Proverbs 26:20.

Where there is no vision, the people perish.
—*Proverbs* 29:18.

O Lord, our Lord, how excellent is thy name in all the earth!

* * *

When I consider thy heavens, the work of thy fingers; the moon and the stars, which thou hast ordained;

What is man, that thou are mindful of him? and the son of man, that thou visitest him?

For thou hast made him a little lower than the angels, and hast crowned him with glory and honour.

Thou madest him to have dominion over the works of thy hands: thou hast put all things under his feet:

* * *

O Lord, our Lord, how excellent is thy name in all the earth! —*Psalms* 8.

The law of the Lord is perfect, converting the soul: the testimony of the Lord is sure, making wise the simple:

The statutes of the Lord are right, rejoicing the heart: the commandment of the Lord is pure, enlightening the eyes:

The fear of the Lord is clean, enduring for

ever: the judgments of the Lord are true and righteous altogether.

More to be desired are they than gold, yea, than much fine gold; sweeter also than honey and the honeycomb.

Let the words of my mouth, and the meditation of my heart, be acceptable in thy sight, O Lord, my strength and my redeemer.

—*Psalms* 19:7-10, 14.

The Lord is my shepherd; I shall not want.

He maketh me to lie down in green pastures: he leadeth me beside the still waters.

He restoreth my soul: he leadeth me in the paths of righteousness for his name's sake.

Yea, though I walk through the valley of the shadow of death, I will fear no evil for thou art with me; thy rod and thy staff they comfort me.

Thou preparest a table before me in the presence of mine enemies: thou anointest my head with oil; my cup runneth over.

Surely goodness and mercy shall follow me all the days of my life: and I will dwell in the house of the Lord for ever.   —*Psalms* 23.

The earth is the Lord's, and the fulness thereof; the world and they that dwell therein.

For he hath founded it upon the seas, and established it upon the floods.

Who shall ascend into the hill of the Lord? or who shall stand in his holy place?

He that hath clean hands, and a pure heart; who hath not lifted up his soul unto vanity, nor sworn deceitfully.

He shall receive the blessing from the Lord.
—*Psalms* 24:1-5.

The Lord is my light and my salvation; whom shall I fear? The Lord is the strength of my life; of whom shall I be afraid?   —*Psalms* 27:1.

Many sorrows shall be to the wicked: but he that trusteth in the Lord, mercy shall compass him about.

Be glad in the Lord, and rejoice, ye righteous: and shout for joy, all ye that are upright in heart.
—*Psalms* 32:10-11.

Keep thy tongue from evil, and thy lips from speaking guile.

Depart from evil, and do good; seek peace, and pursue it.

The eyes of the Lord are upon the righteous, and his ears are open unto their cry.

The face of the Lord is against them that do evil, to cut off the remembrance of them from the earth.

The righteous cry, and the Lord heareth, and delivereth them out of all their troubles.

The Lord is nigh unto them that are of a broken heart; and saveth such as be of a contrite spirit.

Many are the afflictions of the righteous: but the Lord delivereth him out of them all.

—*Psalms* 34:13-19.

O Lord, thou hast searched me, and known me.

Thou knowest my downsitting and mine uprising; thou understandest my thought afar off.

Thou compassest my path and my lying down, and art acquainted with all my ways.

For there is not a word in my tongue, but, lo, O Lord, thou knowest it altogether.

Thou hast beset me behind and before, and laid thine hand upon me.

Such knowledge is too wonderful for me; it is high, I cannot attain unto it.

Whither shall I go from thy Spirit? or whither shall I flee from thy presence?

If I ascend up into heaven, thou art there: if I make my bed in hell, behold, thou art there.

If I take the wings of the morning, and dwell in the uttermost parts of the sea;

Even there shall thy hand lead me, and thy right hand shall hold me.

If I say, Surely the darkness shall cover me; even the night shall be light about me.

Yea, the darkness hideth not from thee: but the night shineth as the day: the darkness and the light are both alike to thee. —*Psalms* 139:1-12.

Awake, my soul! No longer droop in sin. Rejoice, O my heart, and give place no more for the enemy of my soul.

Do not anger again because of mine enemies. Do not slacken my strength because of mine afflictions.

Rejoice, O my heart, and cry unto the Lord, and say: O Lord, I will praise thee forever; yea, my soul will rejoice in thee, my God, and the rock of my salvation.

O Lord, wilt thou redeem my soul? Wilt thou deliver me out of the hands of mine enemies? Wilt thou make me that I may shake at the appearance of sin?

O Lord, wilt thou encircle me around in the robe of thy righteousness! O Lord, wilt thou make a way for mine escape before mine enemies! Wilt thou make my path straight before me! Wilt thou not place a stumbling block in my way—but that thou wouldst clear my way before me, and hedge not up my way, but the ways of mine enemy.

O Lord, I have trusted in thee, and I will trust in thee forever. I will not put my trust in the arm of flesh; for I know that cursed is he that putteth his trust in the arm of flesh.

—*II Nephi* 4:28-34.

RELIGION

WHAT IS RELIGION?

Religion is being honest seven days in the week,
Expressed in thought and action, and in the words
you speak.
It is loving God and neighbor, and serving them
each day;
It's in the way and manner, and not in the times
you pray.
It is treating others squarely, and living the Golden
Rule,

Learning all the lessons given in life's great
school.

—Anonymous.

REPROVING ADVICE

"It was my custom in my youth," says a celebrated Persian writer, "to rise from my sleep, to
watch, pray, and read the Koran. One night, as I
was thus engaged, my father, a man of practiced
virtue, awoke. 'Behold,' said I to him, 'thy children
are lost in irreligious slumbers, while I alone wake
to praise God.' 'Son of my soul,' said he, 'it is
better to sleep than to wake to remark the faults
of thy brethren.' " —They Tell A Story.

AMERICAN GOODNESS

About 100 years ago, Alexis de Tocqueville,
French politician and writer, visited America, and
wrote a book about the people he learned to know
so well. Among other things, he said this:

"I sought for the greatness and genius of
America in her commodius harbors and her ample
rivers, and it was not there; in her fertile fields and
boundless prairies, and it was not there; in her

rich mines and her vast world commerce, and it was not there. Not until I went to the churches of America and heard her pulpits aflame with righteousness did I understand the secret of her genius and power. America is great because she is good, and if America ever ceases to be good, America will cease to be great."

—*Mutual Moments.*

THE TEN COMMANDMENTS EPITOMIZED

———

1. Thou shalt have no other gods before me.
2. Thou shalt not make unto thee any graven image.
3. Thou shalt not take the name of the Lord in vain.
4. Remember the Sabbath day to keep it holy.
5. Honor thy father and thy mother.
6. Thou shalt not kill.
7. Thou shalt not commit adultery.
8. Thou shalt not steal.
9. Thou shalt not bear false witness.
10. Thou shalt not covet anything that is thy neighbor's.

—*Exodus* 20:3-17.

THE BEATITUDES

Blessed are the poor in spirit: for their's is the kingdom of heaven.

Blessed are they that mourn: for they shall be comforted.

Blessed are the meek: for they shall inherit the earth.

Blessed are they which do hunger and thirst after righteousness: for they shall be filled.

Blessed are the merciful: for they shall obtain mercy.

Blessed are the pure in heart: for they shall see God.

Blessed are the peacemakers: for they shall be called the children of God.

Blessed are they which are persecuted for righteousness' sake: for their's is the kingdom of heaven.

Blessed are ye, when men shall revile you, and persecute you, and shall say all manner of evil against you falsely, for my sake.

Rejoice, and be exceeding glad: for great is your reward in heaven: for so persecuted they the prophets which were before you.

—Matt. 5:3-12.

REVERENCE

Profaneness is a low, groveling vice. He who indulges in it is no gentleman. I care not what his stamp may be in society—I care not what clothes he wears or what culture he boasts—despite all his refinement, the light and habitual taking of God's name in vain betrays a coarse nature and a brutal will.   —*E. H. Chapin.*

Religion is the tie that connects man to his Creator, and holds him to His throne.
                              —*Daniel Webster.*

O Father, haste the promised hour,
  When at His feet shall lie
All rule, and authority and power
  Beneath the ample sky;
When He shall reign from pole to pole,
The Lord of every human soul;

When all shall heed the words He said
  Amid their daily cares,
And by the loving life He led
  Shall seek to pattern theirs.
And he who conquered death shall win
The nobler conquest over sin.
                    —*William Cullen Bryant.*

Whoever considers the study of anatomy, I believe, will never be an atheist. The frame of a man's body and the coherence of his parts are so strange and paradoxical that I hold him to be the greatest miracle of Nature. —*Lord Herbert.*

Henceforth my heart shall sigh no more
For olden time and holier store;
God's love and blessing then and there,
Are now, and here, and everywhere.
—*Whittier.*

REWARDS OF RIGHTEOUS LIVING

For thus saith the Lord—I the Lord, am merciful and gracious unto those who fear me, and delight to honor those who serve me in righteousness and in truth unto the end.

Great shall be their reward and eternal shall be their glory.

And to them will I reveal all mysteries, yea, all the hidden mysteries of my kingdom from days of old, and for ages to come, will I make known unto them the good pleasure of my will concerning all things pertaining to my kingdom.

Yea, even the wonders of eternity shall they

know, and things to come will I show them, even
the things of many generations.

And their wisdom shall be great, and their
understanding reach to heaven; and before them
the wisdom of the wise shall perish, and the
understanding of the prudent shall come to
naught.

For by my Spirit will I enlighten them, and by
my power will I make known unto them the
secrets of my will—yea, even those things which
eye has not seen, nor ear heard, nor yet entered
into the heart of man.   —D. & C. 76:5-10.

Now the Lord had shown unto me, Abraham,
the intelligences that were organized before the
world was; and among all these there were many
of the noble and great ones;

And God saw these souls that they were good,
and he stood in the midst of them, and he said:
These I will make my rulers: for he stood among
those that were spirits, and he saw that they
were good; and he said unto me: Abraham, thou
art one of them; thou wast chosen before thou
wast born.

And there stood one among them that was
like unto God, and he said unto those who were

with him: We will go down, for there is space there, and we will take of these materials, and we will make an earth whereon these may dwell;

And we will prove them herewith, to see if they will do all things whatsoever the Lord their God shall command them;

And they who keep their first estate shall be added upon; and they who keep not their first estate shall not have glory in the same kingdom with those who keep their first estate; and they who keep their second estate shall have glory added upon their heads for ever and ever.

—*P. of G. P., Ab.* 3:22-26.

For the day cometh that the Lord shall utter his voice out of heaven; the heavens shall shake and the earth shall tremble, and the trump of God shall sound both long and loud, and shall say to the sleeping nations: Ye saints arise and live; ye sinners stay and sleep until I shall call again.

—*D. & C.* 43:18.

And it came to pass in the thirty and sixth year, the people were all converted unto the Lord, upon all the face of the land, both Nephites and Lamanites, and there were no contentions and disputations among them, and every man did deal justly one with another.

And they had all things common among them; therefore there were not rich and poor, bond and free, but they were all made free, and partakers of the heavenly gift.

And it came to pass that there was no contention in the land, because of the love of God which did dwell in the hearts of the people.

And there were no envyings, nor strifes, nor tumults, nor whoredoms, nor lyings, nor murders, nor any manner of lasciviousness; and surely there could not be a happier people among all the people who had been created by the hand of God.
—*IV Nephi* 1:2, 3, 15, 16.

And moreover, I would desire that ye should consider on the blessed and happy state of those that keep the commandments of God. For behold, they are blessed in all things, both temporal and spiritual; and if they hold out faithful to the end they are received into heaven, that thereby they may dwell with God in a state of never-ending happiness. O remember, remember that these things are true; for the Lord God hath spoken it.
—*Mosiah* 2:41.

REPENTANCE AND FORGIVENESS

If you are tempted to lose patience with your fellowmen, stop and think how patient God has been with you. *—Anon.*

If we put off repentance another day, we have a day more to repent of and a day less in which to repent. *—Mason.*

"NOT UNDERSTOOD"

O God! that men would see a little clearer,
Or judge less harshly when they cannot see!
O God! that men would draw a little nearer
To one another! They'd then be nearer Thee,
And understood.
—Thomas Bracken.

RICHES

PERSONAL WORTH

My advice is: Marry a man who is a fortune in himself. Houses, lands and large inheritance are well enough, but the wheel of fortune turns so rapidly that through some investment all these in a few years may be gone. There are some things, however, which are a perpetual fortune—good manners, geniality of soul, kindness, intelligence, sympathy, courage, perseverance, industry and whole-heartedness. Marry such a one, and you have married a fortune, whether he has an income of $50,000 a year or an income of $1,000. A bank is secure according to its capital stock, and not to be judged by the deposits for a day or a week. A man is rich according to his sterling qualities, and not according to the mutability of circumstances, which may leave with him a large amount of resources today and withdraw them tomorrow. If a man is worth nothing but money, he is poor indeed. If a man has upright character, he is rich. Property may come and go; he is independent of the markets. Nothing can buy him out; nothing can sell him out. He may have more money one year than another, but his better fortunes never vacillate.   —*Talmage*.

A miser grows rich by seeming poor; an extravagant man grows poor by seeming rich.
                                        —*Shenstone*.

If the pursuit of riches were a commendable pursuit, I would join in it, even if I had to become a chariot-driver for the purpose. But seeing that it is not a commendable pursuit, I engage in those which are more to my taste.

—*"Wisdom of the Chinese."*

THE USE OF RICHES

———

I can not call riches better than the baggage of virtue. The Roman word is better—impedimenta. For as the baggage is to an army, so is riches to virtue. It can not be spared or left behind, but it hindereth the march. Yea, and the care of it sometimes loseth or disturbeth victory. Of great riches there is no real use, except it be in the distribution; the rest is but conceit. —*Bacon.*

He that holds fast the golden mean
And lives contentedly between
  The little and the great,
Feels not the wants that pinch the poor,
Nor the plagues that haunt the rich man's door.
—*William Cowper.*

"THE THINGS THAT ARE MORE EXCELLENT"

———

To hug the wealth ye cannot use,
  And lack the riches all may gain—
O blind and wanting wit to choose,
  Who house the chaff and burn the grain!
And still doth life with starry towers
  Lure to the bright, divine ascent!
Be yours the things ye would; be ours
  The things that are more excellent.

The grace of friendship—mind and heart
  Linked with their fellow heart and mind;
The gains of science, gifts of art;
  The sense of oneness with our kind;
The thirst to know and understand—
  A large and liberal discontent:
These are the goods in life's rich hand,
  The things that are more excellent.
                              —*William Watson.*

In this world it is not what we take up but
what we give up that makes us rich.
                              —*Henry Ward Beecher.*

WHAT MONEY CANNOT DO

Money, no doubt, is a power; but a power of well defined and narrow limits. It will purchase plenty, but not peace; it will furnish your table with luxuries, but not you with an appetite to enjoy them; it will surround your sick bed with physicians, but not restore health to your sickly frame; it will encompass you with a cloud of flatterers, but never procure you one true friend.
—*Guthrie.*

Seek not for riches but for wisdom, and behold, the mysteries of God shall be unfolded unto you, and then shall you be made rich. Behold, he that hath eternal life is rich.   —*D. & C.* 6:7.

THE DUTY OF THE RICH

If any man is rich and powerful, he comes under that law of God by which the higher branches must take the burning of the sun, and shade those that are lower; by which the tall trees must protect the weak plants beneath them.   —*Beecher.*

Dug from the mountainside, washed in the glen,
Servant am I, or the master of men;
    Steal me, I curse you,
    Earn me, I bless you,
Grasp me and hoard me, a fiend shall possess you;
Lie for me, die for me, covet me, take me,
Angel or devil, I am what you make me.

                        —Anonymous.

SALVATION AND EXALTATION

The Gospel of Christ is termed by St. Paul, "the power of God unto salvation." Paul might have gone further, had he been so inclined, or had it been timely. He could have shown that the Gospel is also the power of God unto exaltation, a plan devised by omnipotent wisdom whereby the sons and daughters of Deity may advance from stage to stage of soul development, until they become like their heavenly parents, the Eternal Father and Mother, inheriting endless thrones and dominions and receiving a "Fullness of joy."

                        —Orson F. Whitney.

SUCCESS

This book of the law shall not depart out of thy mouth; but thou shalt meditate there in day and night, that thou mayest observe to do according to all that is written therein: for then thou shalt make thy way prosperous, and then thou shalt have good success. —*Joshua* 1:8.

DON'T BE A KNOCKER

Knocking is one of the easiest things in the world to do. It only takes a thimblefull of brains. And it is the cheapest and easiest way to attract attention. But it is a mighty expensive amusement. Everybody hates a knocker.

No man ever got very high by pulling other people down. The intelligent merchant does not knock his competitors. The sensible worker does not knock those who work with him. Don't knock your friends. Don't knock your enemies. Don't knock yourself.

Don't say cutting things. Speak pleasantly of everybody whether you are pleasantly disposed or not. Boost and you will be boosted. Knock and you will be knocked. —*Dr. Frank Crane.*

The men whom I have seen succeed best in life have always been cheerful and hopeful men, who went about their business with a smile on their faces, and took the changes and chances of this mortal life like men, facing rough and smooth alike as it came.   —*Charles Kingsley.*

HOW IMPROVEMENT COMES

If harps of life vibrate discordant tones,
    They need not be the signals of retreat;
Our yesterdays should be the stepping stones
    On which we firmly place our climbing feet.

Improvement comes to neither men nor nations,
    Unless they turn their faces to the light,
And those who reach the highest ranks and stations
    Are always in the thickest of the fight.

                      —*Anonymous.*

THE BETTER CHANCE

Not all the earnest men achieve
    The splendid height where glory dwells,
But worthiness need never grieve
    If folly passes wearing bells.

The vain grow fretful and rebel,
　While merit's patience must be strong;
A man may lose in doing well;
　He cannot win by going wrong.
—S. E. Kiser.

Success in life depends upon staying power. The reason for failure in most cases is lack of perseverance. Men get tired and give up. —J. R. Miller.

Good deeds from good intentions flow; but good intentions only, build for us a place below.
—Anon.

THRIFT

Believe me when I tell you that thrift of time will repay you in after life with a usury of profit beyond your most sanguine dreams, and that the waste of it will make you dwindle, alike in intellectual and in moral stature, beyond your darkest reckonings.   —Gladstone.

What maintains one vice would bring up two children. Remember, many a little makes a mickle; and further, beware of little expenses. A small leak will sink a great ship.   —Franklin.

TRUTH—HONESTY

And when ye shall receive these things, (the Book of Mormon) I would exhort you that ye would ask God, the Eternal Father, in the name of Christ, if these things are not true; and if ye shall ask with a sincere heart, with real intent, having faith in Christ, he will manifest the truth of it unto you, by the power of the Holy Ghost.

And by the power of the Holy Ghost ye may know the truth of all things.   —*Moroni* 10:4-5.

And now, verily I say unto you, I was in the beginning with the Father, and am the Firstborn;

* * *

Ye were also in the beginning with the Father; that which is Spirit, even the Spirit of truth;

And truth is the knowledge of things as they are, and as they were, and as they are to come.

—*D. & C.* 93:21-24.

LOVE THE TRUTH

He who loves will love truth not less than men. He will rejoice in the truth—rejoice not in what he has been taught to believe; not in this church's doctrine or in that; not in this ism or in that

ism; but in the truth. He will accept only that
which is real; he will strive to get at facts; he will
search for truth with a humble and unbiased
mind, and cherish whatever he finds at any
sacrifice.   —*Henry Drummond.*

Truth crushed to earth, shall rise again;
The eternal years of God are hers;
But Error, wounded, writhes in pain,
And dies among her worshipers.
                    —*William Cullen Bryant.*

Last eve I paused beside a blacksmith's door
And heard the anvil ring the vesper chime;
Then, looking in, I saw upon the floor
Old hammers worn with beating years of time.

"How many anvils have you had?" said I,
"To wear and batter all these hammers, so?"
"Just one," said he; then said, with twinkling eye,
"The anvil wears the hammers out, you know."

And so, I thought, the anvil of God's word
For ages skeptic blows have beat upon:
Yet, though the noise of falling blows was heard
The anvil is unharmed—the hammers, gone.
                    —*Anonymous.*

We acknowledge but one motive—to follow the truth as we know it, whithersoever it may lead us; but in our heart of hearts we are well assured that the truth which has made us free, will in the end make us glad also.   —*Adler*.

VALUES OF LIFE

THE VALUES OF LIFE

A gentleman of Boston, an intimate friend of Professor Aga Agassiz, once expressed his wonder that a man of such abilities as he (Agassiz) possessed should remain contented with such a moderate income. "I have enough," was Agassiz's reply. "I have not *time* to make money. Life is not sufficiently long to enable a man to get rich, and do his duty to his fellow-men at the same time." Christian, have you time to serve God and yet to give your whole soul to gaining wealth? The question is left for conscience to answer.

—*Spurgeon*.

BETTER THAN GOLD

Better than grandeur, better than gold,
Than rank and title a thousand fold,
Is a healthy body, a mind at ease,
And simple pleasures that always please;

Better than gold is a conscience clear,
Though toiling for bread in an humble sphere;
Doubly blest with content and health,
Untried by the lusts or cares of wealth.

Better than gold is the sweet repose
Of the sons of toil when their labors close;
Better than gold is the poor man's sleep;
And the balm that drops on his slumbers deep.

Better than gold is a thinking mind
That in the realm of books can find
A treasure surpassing Australian ore,
And live with the great and good of yore.

Better than gold is a peaceful home,
Where all the fireside charities come—
The shrine of love and the heaven of life,
Hallowed by mother, or sister or wife.

However humble the home may be,
Or tried with sorrow by Heaven's decree,
The blessings that never were bought or sold,
And center there, are better than gold.
                              —*Alexander Smart.*

The real values of life are solid and unshakeable. A financial crisis can rob us of all that we have, but it cannot affect what we are.
                              —*Claiborne Johnson.*

THINGS THAT COUNT

Not what we have, but what we use,
Not what we see, but what we choose—
These are the things that mar or bless
The sum of human happiness.

The things near by, not things afar,
Not what we seem, but what we are—
These are the things that make or break
That give the heart its joy or ache.

Not what seems fair, but what is true,
Not what we dream, but what we do—
These are the things that shine like gems,
Like stars in fortune's diadems.
                              —*Anonymous.*

Even if we gave "everything" to secure eternal life, we still have made the most wonderful bargain in the world. William James said: "The greatest use of life is to spend it for something that outlasts it." Eternal exaltation lasts forever and is the greatest possible good.   —*Anonymous.*

VALUES

So often folks have wondered why
  God has placed on earth
The storms, the tears, the raging seas—
  Destroyers of all worth.
But if it weren't for angry skies,
  The torrents, and dismay,
How could we realize the worth
  Of sunny, cloudless day?

                    —*James D. Rogers.*

EVERYTHING COUNTS

Every hardship, every joy, every temptation is a challenge of the spirit, that the human soul may prove itself. The great chain of necessity wherewith we are bound has divine significance, and nothing happens which has not some service to perform in working out the sublime destiny of the human soul.   —*Elias A. Ford.*

WICKEDNESS—SIN

. . . all men that are in . . . a carnal state, are in
the gall of bitterness and in the bonds of iniquity;
they are without God in the world, and they have
gone contrary to the nature of God; therefore, they
are in a state contrary to the nature of happiness.
. . . Behold, I say unto you, wickedness never
was happiness.   —*Alma* 41:10-11.

DANGER IN LITTLE SINS

———

Be fearful of little sins. Take alarm at even an
evil thought, wish or desire. These are the germs
of sin—the floating seeds which drop into the
heart, and, finding in our natural corruption a fat
and favorable soil, spring up into actual trans-
gressions. These, like the rattle of the snake and
the hiss of the serpent, reveal the presence and
near neighborhood of danger. The experience of
all good men proves that sin is most easily crushed
in the bud, and that it is safer to flee from
temptation than to fight it.   —*Guthrie.*

THE GENESIS OF SIN

Do you suffer your thoughts to tamper with evil, and to dally with wrong-doing? If so, you are not sincere. God will regard your thoughts, for *thoughts are heard in heaven*. If you willingly sin in thought, if you are base and guilty there, because you think that no eye will see your thoughts, the guilt and the baseness will sooner or later break into the outlets of word and deed—from thought to wish—from wish to purpose—from purpose to word—from word to act—from act to habit—from delight in the imagination to consent in the will—from consent in the will to guilt in the deed—from deed to repeated transgression, such is the genesis of sin.   —*F. W. Farrar*.

THE AWFULNESS OF SIN

The awfulness of sin comes not wholly from the fact that it is a disobedience of God, but as well from the certainty that it is a doing of violence to the soul itself in the loss of power, the decay of love, the enfeebling of will and the general atrophy of the nature. The thing affected by our indulgence is not alone the book of final judgment, but the present fabric of the spirit.

—Henry Drummond.

"Truly has it been said, that all that is necessary for the triumph of evil is for good men to do nothing."

Sin has many tools, but a lie is a handle which fits them all.   *—Holmes.*

Conscience is the voice of the soul; the passions are the voice of the body.   *—Rousseau.*

Prosperity doth best discover vice; but adversity doth best discover virtue.   *—Bacon.*

PROFANITY

I pity the man who steals when he is hungry or when poverty is pinching his family. I can understand the power of the temptation to which he yields. I have sympathy for the man who drinks when a demon of thirst is at his throat and every drop of blood seems to be calling for rum. But the man who *swears* bites at a bare hook, and goes to hell like a fool.   *Dr. S. F. Upham.*

THE PRICE OF A DRINK

———

"Give me a drink! I will give you my hard earnings for it. Give me a drink! I will pay for it. I will give you more than that. I married a wife; I took her from her girlhood's home, and promised to love and cherish her, and protect her. Ah! Ah! And I have driven her out to work for me, and I have stolen her wages, and I have brought them to you. Give me a drink and I will give you them. More yet. I have snatched the bit of bread from the white lips of my famished child. I will give you that if you will give me a drink. More yet. I will give—I will give you my hopes of heaven—body and soul. I will barter jewels worth all the kingdoms of the earth—for what will a man give in exchange for his soul?—for a dram. Give it me!"

—*J. B. Gough.*

Do not consider any vice as trivial, and therefore practice it; do not consider any virtue as unimportant, and therefore neglect it.

—*"Wisdom of the Chinese."*

WOMAN

A SLOVENLY WOMAN

The most disgusting thing on earth is a slaternly woman. I mean, a woman who never combs her hair until she goes out, or looks like a fright until somebody calls. That man married to one of these creatures stays at home as little as possible is no wonder. It is a wonder that such a man does not go on a whaling voyage of three years, and in a leaky ship. Costly wardrobe is not required; but, O woman, if you are not willing, by all that ingenuity of refinement can effect, to make yourself attractive to your husband, you ought not to complain if he seek in other society those pleasant surroundings which you deny him.

—*Talmage.*

TALMAGE'S MOTHER

My opinion is that the woman who can reinforce her husband in the work of life and rear her children for positions of usefulness is doing more for God and the race and her own happiness than if she spoke on every great platform and headed a hundred great enterprises. My mother never made a missionary speech in her life, and at a missionary meeting I doubt whether she could have got enough courage to vote aye or no; but she raised her son John, who has been preaching the Gospel and translating religious literature in Amoy, China, for about forty years. Was not that a better thing to do? *—Talmage.*

"An honest man is the best thing on the sod; but a mother and her babe is the noblest work of God."

A WOMAN'S PRAYER

O Lord, who knowest every need of mine,
Help me to bear each cross and not repine;
Grant me fresh courage every day,
Help me to do my work alway
    Without complaint!

O Lord, Thou knowest well how dark the way,
Guide Thou my footsteps, lest they stray;
Give me fresh faith for every hour,
Lest I should ever doubt Thy power
    And make complaint!

Give me a heart, O Lord, strong to endure,
Help me to keep it simple, pure,
Make me unselfish, helpful, true
In every act, whate'er I do,
    And keep content!

Help me to do my woman's share,
Make me courageous, strong to bear
Sunshine or shadow in my life!
Sustain me in the daily strife
    To keep content!   —*Anonymous*.

Woman was not taken from the head of man,
for she was not intended to be his ruler; nor from
his feet, for she was not intended to be his slave;
but from his side for she was to be his companion.
                            —*Tertullian*.

THE ARMY AND THE GUNS

———

She's but a slip of womanhood
    One third my weight and size—
Somehow, her spine is stiffer
    And she has two steady eyes.
I'm but the scout—the vanguard—
    Good when opposition runs,
But she's the force behind me—
    She's the "army" and the "guns."

When foemen press the hardest
  I halt and rest awhile
Until I feel her presence,
  See her optimistic smile;
And then I club my musket,
  Ammunition being gone,
And smash our way through troubles,
  And the "army" shoves me on.

For years we've been campaigning—
  Always by the blaze at night
We salve our wounds and bruises
  As we plan the morrow's fight.
I might have furled our colors—
  But the "army" through brave tears
Trenched-in and held the sector
  Through some mighty trying years.

I'm out in front where people
  Think I'm wonderful and brave,
Because I have the banner
  And, of course, they see it wave.
But I'm not fooled by plaudits—
  Scouts and vanguards may look gay,
But when it comes to battles,
  Sure, the "army" wins, alway!

                    —*Harrison R. Merrill.*

A WOMAN'S QUESTION

———

Do you know you have asked for the costliest thing
  Ever made by the Hand above—
A woman's heart and a woman's life,
  And a woman's wonderful love?
Do you know you have asked for this priceless
    thing
  As a child might ask for a toy?
Demanding what others have died to win,
  With the reckless dash of a boy.

You have written my lesson of duty out,
  Manlike, you have questioned me;
Now stand at the bar of a woman's soul
  Until I shall question thee.
You require your mutton shall always be hot,
  Your socks and your shirt shall be whole;
I require your heart shall be true as God's stars,
  As pure as heaven your soul.

You require a cook for your mutton and beef;
  I require a far better thing;
A seamstress you're wanting for stockings and
    shirts—
  I look for a man and a king.

A king for a beautiful realm called home,
　　And a man that the maker, God,
Shall look upon as He did the first,
　　And say "It is very good."

I am fair and young, but the roses will fade
　　From my soft young cheek one day;
Will you love me, then, 'mid the falling leaves,
　　As you did 'mid the bloom of May?
Is your heart an ocean so wide and deep
　　I may launch my all on its tide?
A loving woman finds heaven or hell
　　On the day she is made a bride.

I require all things that are grand and true,
　　All things that a man should be;
If you would give this all, I would stake my life
　　To be all that you demand of me.
If you cannot do this, a laundress and cook
　　You can hire with little pay;
But a woman's heart and a woman's life
　　Are not to be won that way.

—Elizabeth Barrett Browning.

WORK—INDUSTRY

Thank God every morning when you get up that you have something to do that day which must be done, whether you like it or not. Being forced to work and forced to do your best will breed in you temperance and self control, diligence and strength of will, cheerfulness and content, and a hundred virtues which the idle never know.

—*Charles Kingsley.*

LABOR IS GENIUS

———

When a lady once asked Turner, the celebrated English painter, what his secret was, he replied: "I have no secret, madam, but hard work. This is the secret that many never learn, and they do not succeed because they do not learn it. Labor is the genius which changes the world from ugliness to beauty and the great curse to a blessing."

—*Anonymous.*

You never will be saved *by* works; but let us tell you most solemnly that you never will be saved *without* works.   —*T. L. Cuyler.*

Thou shalt not be idle; for he that is idle shall
not eat the bread nor wear the garments of the
laborer.   —*D. & C.* 42:42.

It is not work that kills men; it is worry. Work
is healthy; you can hardly put more upon a man
than he can bear. Worry is rust upon the blade. It
is not the revolution that destroys the machinery
but the friction. Fear secretes acids; but love and
trust are sweet juices.   —*Henry Ward Beecher.*

KEEP A-GOIN'

If you strike a thorn or rose,
  Keep a-goin'!
If it hails or if it snows,
  Keep a-goin'!
'Taint no use to sit an' whine
When the fish ain't on your line;
Bait your hook an' keep a-tryin'—
  Keep a-goin'!

When the weather kills your crop,
  Keep a-goin'!
Though 'tis work to reach the top,
  Keep a-goin'!

S'pose you're out o' ev'ry dime,
Gittin' broke ain't any crime;
Tell the world you're feelin' prime—
    Keep a-goin'!

When it looks like all is up,
    Keep a-goin'!
Drain the sweetness from the cup,
    Keep a-goin'!
See the wild birds on the wing,
Hear the bells that sweetly ring,
When you feel like sighin', sing—
    Keep a-goin'!
                    —*Frank L. Stanton.*

SENTENCE SERMONS OF DR. KARL G. MAESER

We go to the East for learning; but the East will come to the West for wisdom.

No righteous rules, however rigid, are too stringent for me; I will live above them.

Eagerness to earn bread and butter has overshadowed many a golden opportunity.

I would rather trust my child to a serpent than to a teacher who does not believe in God.

All our prayers are addressed in the handwriting of the heart, readable to God and ourselves alone.

Youth demands recreation, and if it is not provided in high places they will seek it in low places.

The truly educated man will always speak to the understanding of the most unlearned of his audience.

If you learn only the fraction of the A of a principle, practice at once that fraction you have learned.

What we did before we came here conditioned us here; what we do here will condition us in the world to come.

It is our privilege to be so fastened to our line of duty that we cannot be turned away by the strongest current of temptation.

Every one of you, sooner or later, must stand at the forks of the road, and choose between personal interest and some principle of right.

If you want excuses, go to the Devil—he can give you any number of them.

Infidelity is consumption of the soul.

Be yourself, but always your better self.

The Lord never gets in debt to any man.

The Lord never does anything arbitrarily.

Make the man within you your living ideal.

Everyone's life is an object lesson to others.

My word shall always be as good as my bond.

Don't be a scrub.

Authority must be an iron fist in a velvet glove.

Say to your soul: "Let no unclean thing enter here."

One who has lost the Spirit of the Lord is spiritually dead.

Let your first good morning be to your Heavenly Father.

A man without character is like a ship without a rudder.

I would rather lose my right arm than break my word of honor.

If it shall please my Heavenly Father, I will be a teacher in heaven.

A laudable ambition to excell is an indispensable requisite to success.

When I listen to a sermon, I have my ears open to the doctrine only.

No man shall be more exacting of me or my conduct than I am of myself.

He that cheats another is a knave; but he that cheats himself is a fool.

Our patriarchal blessings are paragraphs from the book of our possibilities.

—Dr. Karl G. Maeser.